INGATONE
AND
FRYERNING:
a history

The Chequers mosaic, showing Elizabeth I

INGATESTONE
AND
FRYERNING:
a history

Ian Yearsley

Ian Henry Publications

ISNB 0 86025 481 X

Printed by
Interprint, Ltd.
Malta
for
Ian Henry Publications, Ltd
20 Park Drive, Romford, Essex RM1 4LH

INTRODUCTION

The idea of writing a book about Ingatestone has probably been with me since childhood. I was born in the village and although I was destined to grow up outside it, I have nevertheless always regarded it as my spiritual home.

It soon became apparent to me, however, that I would not be able to write about Ingatestone in isolation: neighbouring Fryerning would have to be included, too. For centuries the boundaries of the two parishes were interlinked - to the extent that three quarters of Ingatestone High Street was once in Fryerning parish - so, in historical terms, and, I believe, in community terms too, the two settlements were, and are, truly inseparable. I make no apologies, therefore, for writing about the two parishes together, though Ingatestone, the more important and more bustling of the two, may necessarily take prominence at certain stages.

The history of Ingatestone in particular is a rich and colourful tapestry. Kings, queens, politicians, diarists, market traders and fair owners have all been brought to or through the village by the old Roman highway - the 'Essex Great Road' - that led from London to Colchester. Twenty-three miles from the Capital - a day's horse ride - the village offered an ideal stopping point for travellers bound further afield who could find food and shelter for themselves and their animals in the village inns and stables.

As road traffic increased and wheeled vehicles came into greater use the fortunes of the village grew in parallel. A market and a fair were established, the coaching inns prospered and local farmers were able to take advantage of the constant through-traffic to transport their agricultural produce to the London markets and beyond.

With the arrival of the railway in the mid-19th century, however, much of the traffic bypassed the town and it suffered a temporary decline in prosperity. Later, when the motor car appeared, the village thronged with traffic again, particularly coach traffic heading for the coast, and by 1960 a bypass had been built to take some of this traffic out of the town. In recent years the area has

1

gained a new popularity as a commuter town and prosperity and growth have both followed.

To outsiders, Ingatestone's only real attraction in tourism terms is Ingatestone Hall, built by Sir William Petre (pronounced `Peter') in 1540 and still largely unchanged from that time. Sir William came from Tor Bryan in Devon and his settlement at Ingatestone, handily close to the capital where his work at court often required his attendance, established a branch of the Petre family which continues in the locality to this day.

This is not, it should be stated, the first book to have been written about Ingatestone, but as the last comprehensive study - the last full journey through history from the earliest times to its present day - was (Mrs) E .E. Wilde's 1913 publication, *Ingatestone and the Essex Great Road, with Fryerning,* an update on the story is perhaps a little overdue. More recent books have tended to concentrate on particular facets of village life - principally biographies of various members of the Petre family and studies of the architectural and historical significance of Ingatestone Hall - and have consequently not provided a full modern study of the history and life of the village in its entirety. This book seeks to redress the balance a little by building on Mrs Wilde's work, drawing on the more specialised publications that have appeared since her time and bringing the history of the village up to date as the end of the second Millennium draws ever closer.

I hope that this book will be of interest to Ingatestone residents and visitors alike. If it fills some gaps in the reader's knowledge of the place and provides some entertainment in doing so, then hopefully it will have served its purpose.

Finally, I would like to thank the following people for their help while I was researching this book: Mum, Dad, Mick, Lyn, Rit & Ron, Auntie Ida & Uncle Jack, Uncle Alf, Sheila & David Abrey, Percy Hyde, Ken Langford, Thomas Atkinson, Lord Petre, Reverend Philip Coulton, Reverend Canon John Brown, John Woodgate, Fred Feather, Mr Kyprianou of the Heybridge Hotel, the Headteachers of all three Ingatestone schools, Ingatestone & Fryerning Parish

Council, the Great Eastern Railway and the numerous other Ingatestone and Fryerning people who passed invaluable scraps of information to me through the above-named individuals. Thanks also to Alison, for her encouragement and support.

IAN YEARSLEY

Fryerning Lane stones

EARLY HISTORY

The Land & its Ownership

Ingatestone grew up on the what came to be known as the `Essex Great Road' (the old A12 before the bypass was built) at a position that was conveniently a day's horse ride from London. Travellers could stop for food and shelter and to feed and water their horses.

The highway had been a major route since Roman times for travellers between the Capital and East Anglia, passing as it did through such major settlements as Chelmsford, Colchester and Ipswich. Originally little more than a track through the once-extensive Essex Forest, it increased in importance, as many roads did, as people began to move around the country.

At Ingatestone, tracks from the developing path through the forest led off towards the neighbouring villages of Blackmore, Fryerning (to the north west), Buttsbury and Stock (to the south east). Fryerning Lane - now one of the four main roads meeting at the busy crossroads in the middle of the village - was formed a little later than some of the early forest tracks and the original route to Fryerning may well have been via a track in the Whadden Chase area. There has, nevertheless, always been a close relationship between Ingatestone and Fryerning villages and the curious arrangement whereby the two parishes were geographically inter-twined - an arrangement altered only with the parish boundary changes of 1889 - perhaps owed its existence to the field patterns of Saxon days, patterns which may have originated with the Romans.

This part of Essex contains a large number of villages with `ing' naming derivations. These include both Ingatestone and Fryerning themselves, as well as Mountnessing, Margaretting and Ingrave. Historical documents relating to the first of these refer to several `ing' or `ging(e)' settlements within the areas that are now covered by Ingatestone and Fryerning parishes and there is no sure way of telling definitively to which places each document refers. In essence, however, the situation is as set out below.

Ingatestone village takes its name from Ing-atte-stone, `the

4

Stone by Ingatestone church door

people who live at the stone'. This is a Saxon naming derivation, seemingly indicating that there must have been a settlement here in Saxon times. Fragments of the stone from which the village gets its name - fragments which have been variously described as glacial erratics and sarsen stones - can still be seen at the corners of Fryerning Lane and in the churchyard. There is a similar stone on the outskirts of Fryerning - on the Blackmore Road near Woodcock Lodge. An unsubstantiated claim has been made that there may once have been a stone circle on what is now the Recreation Ground, formerly called Stonefield, but there is no evidence to support this. The importance of the stone to early settlers cannot, however, be called into question, since it must have been a piece of significant size to warrant naming the settlement after it.

The importance of this settlement probably increased when the Romans established their road, along the route of the old forest track, from London to Colchester. The typically Roman straight-line of the old road is still very much in evidence from a glance at the map today.

The wider Ingatestone village seems to have evolved from an area known as 'Ging(e) Abbess', so called because it was once the property of the Abbess of Barking Abbey. The Abbey's ownership of land in this area lasted from Saxon times (c.950) until the Dissolution of the Monasteries in 1539. The area is, however, sometimes referred to as 'Ging(e) (ad) Petram', apparently a Latin name referring to the stone.

Barking Abbey, one of the largest and most powerful of the county's religious houses, is said to have been founded in 666 by Erkenwald, later Bishop of London, who was created a saint for his apparently miraculous powers. His sister, Ethelburga, was the first abbess. The Curfew Tower (the Gatehouse) and some stone foundations are the only substantial parts of the Abbey that survive.

At the Dissolution Ingatestone passed into the ownership of Dr (later Sir) William Petre (c.1505-1572), who bought it from the Crown for £849 12s 6d, probably paid in instalments. Sir William, who was later to become a Secretary of State and Privy Councillor

Curfew Tower, Barking

to Henry VIII, played an active role in the Dissolution process. He had special responsibility for visiting monasteries and other similar religious houses and would have known the Ingatestone area well, both from its direct connection with Barking Abbey and also perhaps from visits which he may have made to nearby Thoby Priory in Mountnessing and Jericho Priory in Blackmore (a favourite haunt of Henry VIII). He may well also have been attracted to the place by the similarity of the Latin name for it to his own surname.

Sir William was destined to entertain two monarchs at his new Ingatestone home, Ingatestone Hall, but these were not the first members of the Royal Family to pass through the village. King John may well have ridden on the highway when travelling to his Hunting Lodge at Writtle or, just as likely, when making a well-documented journey between Chelmsford and Faversham in the first decade of the 13th century. Late in the next century Richard II probably used the road when visiting his uncle, the Duke of Gloucester, at Pleshey, as this would have been the most direct route from London.

Ingatestone parish church, dedicated to St Edmund and St Mary, is situated in the centre of the village, right on the Essex Great Road, and would almost certainly have been a place of refuge and rest for pilgrims and other travellers. The dedication derives in part from the East Saxon king killed by the Danes in the 9th century and in part from the parish's association with Barking's St Mary's Abbey. The east window of the south chapel includes some scenes from the life of St Edmund.

While Ingatestone has a strong Barking Abbey connection, only part of neighbouring Fryerning appears to have been in the Abbess's ownership, with the area around the church belonging at the time of the Domesday Survey to the Norman nobleman, Robert Gernon, whose family held a lot of land throughout the county. At one time this area may have been the site of an encampment of the Trinobante people - the earthworks in the churchyard and the establishment of the settlement on high ground, giving good views over land to the south and with easy access to woodland for fuel and dwellings to the north, are thought by some to be evidence of this. Moore's Ditch at nearby Mill Green may have been an ancient earthwork and some ancient local field names contained the word `camp', implying some form of early settlement in the vicinity. The extensive use of Roman bricks in the parish church and a number of Roman finds in the Mill Green area also point to some sort of Roman occupation locally.

Gernon's property at Fryerning passed into the ownership of the Montfitchet family - another well-known landholding family in the county (whose name survives in the town of Stansted Mountfitchet). Part was then given by Gilbert Montfitchet in 1167-8 to the Knights Hospitallers to ensure that prayers would be said for the souls of his parents (though his mother was still alive at the time). The Knights held the land until the Dissolution (c.1540) under the name of `Ging(e) Hospital'. They appear, however, to have at one stage only leased some of it, probably from the Burnel family, who may well have bought back some of the land in order to help the Knights with their finances in the late-13th and early 14th centuries. Their property incorporated the main part of Fryerning, including the church, and it is they who are thought to have been responsible for the construction of the building's impressive brick tower, which is not too dissimilar in style from that at Ingatestone.

When the Knights fell from favour, much of the land at Fryerning passed into the possession of the Berners family, under Sir William Berners, a royal auditor. The Berners were yet another important landholding family in Essex - they held some land locally in Writtle and at Mountnessing's Thoby Priory and their name survives today in the village of Berners Roding. The old Knights Hospitallers' property became known as `Ging(e) Berners' or `Ging(e) Fryerne', the latter name almost certainly deriving from the land's former connection with the friars who were involved with the Knights Hospitallers. Mrs Archibald Christy, writing in a chapter in Mrs Wilde's book of 1913, speculated that there may once have been a small local monastery somewhere in the Beggar Hill-St Leonard's-Furze Hall area of Fryerning, from which the name could also possibly have been derived, but later research has seemed to suggest that this is unlikely.

Whatever the case, the settlement name did begin a slow evolutionary process from `Ging(e) Fryerne', through `Fryerne [or Friar's Ing]' to the modern day `Fryerning'.

Events

In the mid-fourteenth century the Black Death was in Ingatestone and Fryerning, as it was in much of the rest of the country. Neighbouring Buttsbury, whose church now appears to be located miles away from any accompanying settlement, may well have suffered particularly badly at this time, with the houses that were once there disappearing altogether.

The Black Death, the most devastating disease known to man-kind at this period, had worked its way from Weymouth in Dorset in 1348, through London and on to Norfolk by the end of 1349, the year in which it was probably at · its most prevalent in Ingatestone. There was a Pest Field in Stock Lane - in Wilde's day the fourth field on the right beyond the railway bridge - which was used either for the burial of the dead or as a temporary holding place for sick travellers passing through the village. The highway at this period was a dangerous place because it brought travellers to the village who were carriers of the killer disease.

The high number of deaths in the south east caused by the Black Death led to a reduction in the number of labourers available to work on the land. Those who survived asked for, and often got, more money for their work and they were consequently able to move around more freely, in a never-ending search for better rates of pay, in a way that they had previously never been able to do. Landowners naturally objected to their employees' new-found freedom and a law was passed preventing this freedom of movement from taking place.

In 1381 these restrictions, and the imposition of a new Poll Tax (a tax levied on every head), caused the down-trodden labourers to rebel in what became known as the Peasants' Revolt. Essex men were

St Edmund & St Mary, Ingatestone, south-west

amongst the leading protagonists of the revolt and there were major incidents at the nearby towns of Brentwood and Billericay.

After the Revolt had been put down many of those who had been involved were tried at Chelmsford, where it was reported, somewhat colourfully, that "with a weaver of Billerica many men of the vills of Gyng Bokking Gyngattestane rose up against the king and gathered congregations at Brendewoode, and made assault on justices of the peace with bows and arrows to kill them, afterwards they rode about armed in a land of peace, and did many ill deeds".

Seventy years later, during Henry VI's reign, a similar uprising led by Jack Cade, which definitely involved rebels from Ongar, Doddinghurst, Stondon and Great Waltham, may well also have included Ingatestone and Fryerning people.

On a lighter note, the highway also brought more peaceful people to the village - pilgrims travelling either from London and the south to the shrine of Our Lady of Walsingham in Norfolk, or from East Anglia to Brentwood, from where they would head for Tilbury to cross the River Thames *en route* to Canterbury. Many of these pilgrims may well have stopped to worship at Ingatestone church.

Buildings

As with most settlements, the oldest buildings in the two villages are their churches.

The oldest part of Ingatestone church is the north wall of the old Norman nave, dating from the last quarter of the 11th century, though there may well have been a Saxon church on the site long before that. Within 200-300 years, however, Ingatestone had grown into a busy market town and the church had to be enlarged to cope with the growing congregation. The south wall was demolished and a new one built some 14 feet to the south, creating a new south aisle.

By the early 16th century the chancel had been slightly extended and a fine brick tower had been added, built of perhaps half a million locally-made bricks. This tower has been described by

Nikolaus Pevsner, the recognised authority on important historical architecture, as being amongst the most magnificent in the county. A large brick barn at nearby Ingatestone Hall may well have been built at the same time and from the same brickfield.

Sadly the only really ancient items of fittings and fixtures inside the building that have survived are the communion table and a marvellous old iron hourglass stand (used for supporting the hourglass that was once used to time sermons - which had to last for a minimum length of time in those days). This stand is currently on display on the north wall of the nave.

The plaster on this wall hides a number of mediæval paintings (c.1400) which were discovered during a Victorian restoration in the 1860s and then plastered over again. There were probably once several other similar paintings there because a surviving 16th century document gives details of fees for hiring out church land for the grazing of cows - and such fees were used to buy candles to light sacred `images' in the church.

Ingatestone's first known rector was officiating in 1175. All the early appointments were made by Barking Abbey, but little is known of the individual incumbents until the first half of the 16th century.

The oldest part of Fryerning church - the nave and chancel - also dates from the late 11th century. Here, though, the thickness of the walls and the height and narrowness of the original Norman windows both point to the building having originally been used as a place to hide in and defend in times of attack as well as a place of worship. The extensive use of Roman brick in the church's construction has led some to suggest that there might even have been a building there in Roman times.

The church tower is slightly older than that at Ingatestone and is equally as magnificent. Like that of its neighbour it was probably made from local brick, as there is evidence of there once having been a brickfield not far from the church. Brick and pottery manufacturing facilities, including ancient kilns, have also been found at Mill Green, half a mile or so to the north. Pottery and tile kilns thrived in this locality, thanks partly to the locally prevalent

St Mary the Virgin, Fryerning (note Roman bricks in the courses)

clay which made a good natural manufacturing material, partly to the good availability of timber for fuel and partly to the easy accessibility of the London markets, to which goods were sent via the highway through Ingatestone. The name of Potter Row Farm at Mill Green retains a link with this ancient industry.

Apart from its impressive exterior, Fryerning church also has several notable features inside. In the vestry there is a palimpsest brass - one piece of brass with a carving on each side - showing figures from the 15th and 16th centuries respectively. The identity of the 15th century figure (c.1460) is unknown, but the later figure represents Mary Berners, a descendant of the landowner, Sir William Berners. In 1774 a visitor to the church noted that there was also a brass to Mary's husband, Leonard Berners, on display.

The church's ancient font, made of Caen stone, is also of note, both for its great age (12th century) and for the mysterious symbolic carvings on each of its four square sides - all, apparently, ancient sacred symbols. There are similar fonts at churches in the other Essex villages of Abbess Roding and Little Laver. Fryerning also possesses the oldest church bell in the locality - the treble dates from 1590. The rood loft stairs also survive, as they do at Ingatestone.

The first known rector of Fryerning is Robert Caro, instituted in 1361, though ancient records cite Henry de Maldon as chaplain there around 1190.

SIR WILLIAM PETRE & INGATESTONE HALL

From the 1540s onwards the Petre family was to become the most important family in Ingatestone. The arrival of Dr William Petre and the establishment of the family seat at Ingatestone Hall started a branch of the family whose lineage continues In Ingatestone to this day. Various family members have had important court or judicial roles and their associations with Royalty and other VIPs have given Ingatestone a connection with various society notables that it might otherwise never have had.

Dr William Petre hailed from Tor Bryan, some five miles west of Torquay, Devon, and was one of the stars of 16th century politics and diplomacy. Born in about 1505 he was enrolled at Exeter College, Oxford, by 1520. He was elected a Fellow of All Souls by 1523 and had graduated as a Bachelor of Civil and Canon Law by 1526. He became tutor to George Boleyn, brother of Anne, and travelled abroad with George when the latter was ambassador to France. He may even have been involved during this time with seeking learned and religious opinion about Henry VIII's plans to divorce Catherine of Aragon.

In 1533 Petre was back at Oxford as a Doctor of Civil Law. Three years later he was commissioned as deputy to Thomas Cromwell, Henry VIII's Secretary and Vicar-General, where he specialised in ecclesiastical matters. He was also appointed that year as one of the 12 Masters in Chancery, whose head was the Master of the Rolls, and he subsequently became a Visitor of the Monasteries for the King - a rôle which involved him in securing numerous religious houses' surrender and dissolution and resulted in his first acquisition of land and property at Ingatestone.

In 1540 Cromwell lost his influence with the King (over his involvement in the latter's unsuccessful marriage to Anne of Cleves), fell from grace and was executed. Petre, however, retained Henry's favour and became a member of the King's Council. He was also serving in Parliament at around this time (definitely from 1542 onwards) and was a knight of the Shire of his adopted county of Essex for many years.

In January 1544 Petre was appointed as one of Henry's two Principal Secretaries, serving alongside the more senior Sir William Paget. In the same month he was made a member of the Privy Council (the inner body of the King's Council) and also received a knighthood. He effectively became the Secretary of State for Home and Foreign Affairs, War and the Navy.

In 1547 Henry died and was succeeded by his nine-year-old son as Edward VI. The Duke of Somerset, brother of Edward's late mother, Jane Seymour, was chosen as Protector while Edward was a minor. Petre was retained as Secretary, though this time the other Secretary was another Essex man, Thomas Smith of Saffron Walden.

In 1549 the Privy Council set up a committee to oversee the censorship of seditious books - Petre, Smith and William Cecil were given the job. In the same year, Somerset was forced from power by the Duke of Northumberland, who became Protector in his place and took over the reins of government, replacing Smith as Secretary with, first, Nicholas Wotton, and then William Cecil. Petre, as was rapidly becoming typical of him, managed once again to survive the changes and even gained the treasurership of the Court of the First Fruits in addition to his other roles. He also gained substantial credit for negotiating the sale of Boulogne (held at the time by England) to France for an impressive 400,000 crowns.

As time went on Northumberland began to behave tyrannically, appropriating numerous religious endowments for himself and closing schools attached to chantries. Chelmsford Grammar School was one of the few to survive, saved by the influence of Petre who became its senior governor in 1551.

As Edward's health began to fail, the various rival factions for succession to the throne began to make themselves known. Northumberland secured the marriage of his son, Lord Guildford Dudley, to the 17-year-old Lady Jane Grey, whose mother was a grand-daughter of Henry VII, and sought to alter the succession in her favour. He also took the unprecedented step of appointing a

Ingatestone Hall early in the 20th century

third Principal Secretary, Sir John Cheke (Cecil's son-in-law), to help bring his plans to fruition.

In 1553, when Edward died, Jane was proclaimed Queen, but Edward's sister, Mary, daughter of Catherine of Aragon, had a better claim to the throne and more supporters and Jane was deposed after only nine days. Northumberland was charged with treason and executed. Jane, who had been an unwilling Queen and a virtual pawn in Northumberland's fatal political game, was similarly treated.

On her way from Framlingham to London to collect the crown, Mary stopped at Ingatestone Hall. Cecil and Cheke were dismissed as Secretaries, but Petre once again retained his post and was additionally created Chancellor of the Order of the Garter. Sir John Bourne was established as the other Secretary, but Petre was at the peak of his political career at this point and retained almost sole control of foreign and fiscal affairs. He was involved with the negotiation of the marriage treaty between Mary and Philip of Spain and, with Thomas Thirlby (Bishop of Norwich and the Queen's Ambassador), also concluded an important trade agreement between England and Russia. In recognition of all the invaluable service which he had provided, he was given the large and important manor of Writtle (just up the road from Ingatestone) in exchange for some much smaller and less significant West Country landholdings.

In 1557, at the height of his power, Petre resigned as Secretary, to be succeeded by Dr John Boxall. The reasons for his decision are unclear. Ill-health has been suggested, but this is not borne out by his busy activity in subsequent years. His abhorrence of Mary's policy of burning Protestants at the stake (many of them in Essex towns around Ingatestone - at Brentwood and Chelmsford, for example) may well have been the real reason.

Whatever the cause of his resignation, Petre was back on the Council the following year when Elizabeth succeeded her sister, but Cecil (back in favour) was now sole Secretary. Nonetheless, Petre stood in for Cecil for several months when he was away in Scotland negotiating the withdrawal of the French from there and the extinguishing of Mary Queen of Scots' claim to the English throne.

In July 1561 Elizabeth chose to stop at Ingatestone Hall on one of the many Progresses which she took around the country during her reign. This was perhaps the most extravagant visit by a monarch to the locality and must have made quite an impression on those local people who were lucky enough to see her. The main menu during her stay included such delicacies as congers, cygnets, egrets, gurnards, heron, quail, shovellers and sturgeon, plus less exotic but equally important items such as beer and fruit. 'Minor' items included 693 eggs, 14 dishes of butter, 5 gallons of cream, 200 oranges, half a peck of fine white salt and an array of spices. Elizabeth may well have been back at Ingatestone in 1579 - the Progress that year was cut short, perhaps because of the plague, and it is not clear whether or not she actually made the planned visit.

From 1562 onwards Petre began to step out of the political lime-light but he could not make a full withdrawal before a few more tasks had been undertaken. In 1564 he was given temporary charge of Lady Katherine Grey, sister of Lady Jane, who was placed under virtual house arrest at Ingatestone Hall as a result of her decision to marry the Earl of Hertford without the Queen's permission (a treasonable offence, as Katherine would be next in line to the throne under the terms of Henry VIII's will if Elizabeth did not have any children). Katherine evidently got on well with the family for she became godmother to Petre's daughter Thomasine's second son, born while she was staying at the Hall. She also carved her name into the stone chimney-piece in one of the rooms of the house.

Petre's intense and seemingly unrelenting involvement in the nation's affairs did, however, finally begin to decrease throughout the 1560s. 1562 was the last year he was returned to parliament. In 1566 he withdrew almost completely from public life and in 1567 he made his last known appearance at the Privy Council. Ill and ageing, he presumably wanted to spend as much time as he could from then on with his growing family.

Despite his many commitments, Petre somehow found time to get married - and not once, but twice. His first wife (the marriage took place c.1533) was Gertrude (d.1541), daughter of Sir John Tyrell of Little Warley Hall (whose main seat was Heron Hall at East Horndon). His second wife (from 1542 onwards) was Anne Tyrell, first wife of another John Tyrell, a distant cousin of the father of his first wife. Petre's newly acquired estates at Ingatestone, his marriage into an important local family and the proximity of Essex to London all combined to keep him in the county, away from his native Devon, and laid down the roots of a branch of the family that was to continue in the village for many centuries afterwards.

The Petres' home, Ingatestone Hall, must have been a very busy place during Sir William's lifetime. His second wife Anne had brought two children of her own with her from a previous marriage and Petre himself had at least six of his own children from his two marriages, not counting others who may have died in infancy. As far as the histories of Ingatestone and Fryerning are concerned, the most important of his children were Dorothy (b.1535 to his first wife), who was destined to marry Sir Nicholas Wadham, and John (b.1549 to his second wife), who was destined to succeed him. Both are discussed in more detail in later chapters.

Sir William evidently liked having people around him because, apart from his immediate family, he often invited important guests to Ingatestone Hall, such as members of the Tyrell family, with whom he had family connections, or one of his fellow Essex landowners and statesmen, Richard, Lord Rich. The composer, William Byrd, who lived at nearby Stondon Massey and who later became a close friend of Sir William's son John, was another well-known visitor at this period. The Hall was particularly full with such guests at Christmas, a time of the year when Sir William is also known to have held feasts for poor Ingatestone residents from around 1550 onwards. Over the years he also had many children (usually boys) in his care, who came to the Hall to learn good manners and discipline. There were also at least 45 servants present at the Hall at this time, probably more.

Petre's first two acquisitions of land in Essex had been made in 1537, when he leased some land at Great Burstead and bought the Thameside Manor of Bayhouse in West Thurrock, which was conveniently situated for waterborne transport to and from the Capital. With the subsequent acquisition of Ingatestone from Barking Abbey - and land at Dunton and East Horndon which his second wife, Anne, brought with her on their marriage - he began to build up a vast estate in mid- and south Essex which his successors continued to expand.

His own Essex acquisitions after Ingatestone included more land at East Horndon, the manors of Blunts Wall (near Billericay), Crondon (near Stock) and Peldon (near Colchester), parts of Mountnessing (including Thoby Priory), Margaretting, Writtle, Mashbury, Matching, Chignal St Mary and Chignal St James, Friern (in Nevendon), Clavering, Langley, Ingrave, Cranham and Great Bromfords (also in Nevendon). There were also his inherited family lands in the West Country and elsewhere and a selection of town houses in London, notably in Aldersgate Street. By the time of his death he owned almost 45,000 acres - nearly 20,000 of which were in mid- and south Essex.

Petre's busy political and social life in the capital did not, however, ever distract him completely from making a home at Ingatestone. In 1540 he demolished the old Ingatestone Hall - known at the time from its Barking Abbey origins as Abbess Hall - and replaced it with a brand new building, built round a quadrangle in imitation perhaps of some of the monastic buildings which he had visited. His decision to demolish the old house was apparently based on the fact that he thought it to be 'scant meet for a farmer to dwell upon' and he may well have used a monastic architect in the construction of its replacement.

The new building, completed by c.1544, remains largely intact and in its original form, apart from the west wing which was removed c.1800. The Hall is still in the ownership of the Petre family, much of it open to members of the public for viewing in the summer months. A tour of the building takes in the Stone Hall, the Drawing Room, the Study, the Dining Room, His Lordship's Bedroom, The Dressing Room, the Queen Anne Room and the Long Gallery, which contains an excellent collection of pictures and

Ingatestone Hall clock tower

memorabilia related to the house and the Petre family. Original 16th century features can be seen throughout the interior, which is also furnished with a wide selection of furniture and ornaments from various time periods and from various parts of the world. A visitors' book containing the signature of the current Queen Mother shows that Queens Mary and Elizabeth have not been the only Royal visitors to Ingatestone Hall. Queen Mary, the present Queen's grandmother, and Princess Marie-Jose of Belgium (later Queen of Italy) are, however, the only other known Royal visitors.

The grounds of the Hall contain both Cedar and Lime Walks, as well as an orchard, a maze, a lake, a walled garden and - perhaps the most visibly striking feature of the whole estate - a one-handed clock which sits on a tower over the archway through which visitors make their first approach to the Hall. The motto on the clock, *Sans Dieu Rien* [Without God nothing], is the motto of the Petre family. A two-storey brick barn next to the clocktower is also a legacy from Sir William's 16th century building.

For a time during Sir William's occupancy, the grounds of Ingatestone Hall were used as a deer park - a licence was received from the Crown to impark 300 acres of the estate between the Hall and the London-Colchester road. This arrangement, however, lasted only until 1605, the family preferring to obtain their venison from their estate at Crondon Park.

Apart from Ingatestone Hall, the parish church also benefitted from Sir William's patronage as a direct result of his acquiring Ingatestone land at the Dissolution. After taking over ownership from Barking Abbey he was absolved from the Interdict of Excommunication which had been issued by the Pope against Henry VIII and his administration on condition that he founded a charity for the poor. He did this by founding the Ginge Petre Charity and building almshouses in Stock Lane, Ingatestone, for seven poor inhabitants and a priest-in-charge. He endowed the property with lands with a value of £50 per year.

He further cemented this generous benefaction to the local community with the 1556 construction of a new south chapel at

The South Chapel of Ingatestone church, built by Sir William Petre, 1556

Ingatestone church, erected a year before the almshouses opened. On the outside of the east wall of this chapel the initials `WP' and `AP', commemorating William Petre and his second wife Anne, are still just faintly visible, despite being badly weathered over the years. According to his accounts of payments for the chapel, the tilers used 18,500 `of playne tyle & holowtyle' and 1,200 paving tiles. Jackson, the carpenter, was paid £48 2s for his work.

Sir William Petre died in 1572 and was buried in Ingatestone church, where an impressive tomb-chest monument featuring recumbent effigies of both him and his second wife can still be seen. After almost a lifetime of service dedicated to his country he had, incredibly, managed to survive the political intrigues of Tudor life for several decades and had successfully served four successive monarchs without the pain of disgrace, imprisonment, exile or execution that had at one time or another seemingly befallen almost all of his colleagues, peers or masters. That he had been able to achieve this feat is perhaps all the more surprising when one realises that he held strong Catholic sympathies - but his support for this cause never really jeopardised his senior position, despite occurring at a time when Catholicism and Protestantism in England seemed to pass in and out of favour with virtually every change of monarch.

Sir William was clearly a very shrewd and intelligent operator. More significantly for us, he was also the first - and is still arguably the most - important historical figure to have a connection with Ingatestone and Fryerning.

The tomb of Sir William Petre and his wife, Anne

THE LATE 16TH CENTURY

Through his well-developed skills in diplomacy Sir William Petre had managed somehow to maintain his eminent position throughout changing religious circumstances - and despite continuing to give ardent support to the Catholic cause. This support even extended to the provision of so-called `priest-holes', hiding places for Catholic priests, within the walls of his home at Ingatestone Hall. Similar hiding places have been found at Fryerning Hall, of a similar date.

The priest-hole system provided some protection for those seeking refuge from the authorities, usually for their recusant views, but it was never a totally fool-proof method of concealment. At the height of religious persecution, houses were searched for suspects on a regular basis and a determined band of pursuers would more often than not eventually find its man. At Ingatestone the Catholic priest, John Payne, was just one of a number of people throughout the country to be sought out, captured and tried for his religious beliefs.

Payne was one of four Catholic martyrs of this period who had close associations with Essex and was the only one in the county to be executed during Elizabeth's reign. He appears to have been a convert from Protestantism and a one-time steward of Stondon Hall, about five miles from Ingatestone. A `prudent, serious, mature, religious' man, he was ordained in 1576 and went to Ingatestone Hall to be the personal chaplain and steward of Lady Petre, Sir William's widow.

By winter 1576-77 he had already been arrested and imprisoned for his religious beliefs, but he was not incarcerated for long on that occasion. He moved around a great deal for the next few years until 1581, when he was betrayed by a former servant at Ingatestone Hall, George Eliot, who appears to have had something of a track record in Catholic betrayals.

The following year he was taken to Chelmsford for trial and was charged, with no evidence, with trying to persuade Eliot to murder Queen Elizabeth. Eliot was the only witness. Payne was convicted of the crime and hung, drawn and quartered in Chelmsford Market

Place in front of a large partisan crowd. In 1970 Payne was made a saint in the Catholic church with a Chelmsford school and Sir William Petre's Ingatestone almshouses being dedicated to him.

As Payne found out to his cost, this was a dangerous time to have strong views on religion, particularly if they were diametrically opposed to the prevailing views of the monarch and/or authorities of the day. Numerous other local clergymen had to make sacrifices because they made their views known too widely and would not withdraw them. In 1566, for example, the Ingatestone parish rector, John Woodward (who was probably Payne's uncle), resigned his position in protest at church reforms and moved to Ingatestone Hall to be chaplain to the Petre family. His predecessor, John Green, appears to have adopted a lifesaving policy of trimming his sails to whichever religious wind was prevailing at the time. Green is also notable as being the first rector of Ingatestone not to be appointed by Barking Abbey.

At Fryerning in 1587 Ralph Hawkdon (or Hawdon), was indicted at the assizes along with several other Essex rectors for not using a cross during baptism and for failing to wear a surplice. He was subsequently dismissed from office. By comparison, his replacement, William Owen, did remarkably well to survive the changing fashions of the Church at this time, managing to hold on to his incumbency at Fryerning for a commendable 33 years. He was appointed by the patron, Thomas Baker, a local landowner connected through marriage to the Berners family, with whom the Bakers had had a celebrated legal dispute over land ownership in what became known as the Butler & Baker case (a Mary Berners had remarried, for a second time, into the Butler family after her second husband's death).

Reverend Owen, who came to Fryerning from Hatfield Peverel, did not, however, entirely escape a brush with the authorities. On one occasion he was called upon to answer a charge of negligence that "the chancel is decayed, the roof is uncovered so that it raineth in and the people cannot sit there" and at another time his churchwarden was reprimanded for pulling down the old church porch before a new one was erected. Another problem for the rector was the destruction of the parsonage barn in a storm (c.1594).

Owen's Ingatestone contemporary, Antony Brasier, was even more successful in terms of length of service, lasting 43 years from 1566 to 1609. He also held the living at neighbouring Mountnessing for a while, but appears to have used curates in both places to help him out. He was also Canon of Salisbury for much of his time at Ingatestone, so he was evidently a rather busy man. One of the church bells at Ingatestone (dating from 1660) bears the name `Thomas Brasier' - Thomas was probably a descendant of Antony.

In 1572 when Sir William Petre died the extensive Petre estates at Ingatestone and elsewhere passed on to his only surviving son, John Petre (1549-1613). John was never to equal the considerable achievements of his father, but was nevertheless notable for his own contribution to matters of local and regional significance. His biographer, A. C. Edwards, states that he was "never a national figure, but he was a county magnate of considerable eminence, who carried out his public duties seriously and thoroughly."

He was educated at the Middle Temple in the fashion of the day in order to give him a grounding in law and the ways of London society in preparation for his expected duties as a magistrate in the county and the manager of his father's estates. His steward, John Bentley, went with him to London and remained a dependable assistant when the pair returned to Ingatestone.

Married in 1570 and knighted in 1576, John Petre played a leading rôle in local government administration and in the judiciary. He was High Sheriff of Essex in 1575, a knight of the shire from 1584-7 and Deputy Lieutenant 1588-1603. He also had significant responsibilities during the preparations to repel the Spanish Armada in 1588. As a Justice of the Peace in the county he was second only to his friend Sir Thomas Mildmay, who lived at Moulsham, Chelmsford.

Following his marriage - to Mary Waldegrave of Borley (a member of another major Essex landowning family) - John lived for a time at Writtle Park, the estate which had been given to his father by Queen Mary in recognition of the former's invaluable services. In about 1573, however, John bought West Horndon Hall (later referred to as Thorndon Hall) - a 15th century brick building which he extensively altered and enlarged - and moved his family into this new property shortly afterwards.

West Horndon Hall was originally little more than a small, moated, brick-built lodge. In 1414, however, the Welsh vintner, Lewis John, had received a licence from the Crown to embattle and crenellate it, surround it with a wall and impark some 300 acres of the surrounding countryside. In 1455-6 extensive alterations were made, with the construction of a new hall, work being carried out on several rooms and the partial infilling of the moat. This post-alteration 'ancient house of brick, very well leaded being meet for a nobleman to dwell and keep good hospitality upon' was the one which John Petre was to buy from Lewis John's descendant, Lord Mordaunt, in 1573.

Petre then began a series of extensive alterations, lasting from 1575-95, completely remodelling the original 15th century house into 'modern' Elizabethan style. Local labourers and materials were used wherever possible, with large quantities of bricks, tiles, lime and timber all coming from the surrounding countryside and villages. Petre's enthusiasm for the project was never daunted, not even by a massive storm on Twelfth Night in 1590 which damaged the stables, coach houses and outbuildings just as they were nearing completion. The stables had to be completely taken down and rebuilt.

West Horndon had now become the principal seat of the Petre family, even while the restorations were taking place. John Petre himself spent only short times away from it - such as the nine months at Ingatestone Hall from October 1589 to June 1590 when the restoration work at West Horndon was evidently too involved to enable the family to stay there. Old Lady Petre - Sir William's widow - had died in 1581 and John even carried out some work at Ingatestone Hall as well while he was there.

This short, enforced spell away from West Horndon must nevertheless have been pleasurable, as the family returned to

Ingatestone Hall for at least eight out of the next nine Christmases. But the trend had been set and Ingatestone tended thenceforth to be used only by widows or heirs of successive heads of the Petre family, while the head himself lived with his immediate family at West Horndon. It was not, in fact, to be until the early years of the 20th century that Ingatestone Hall once more became the family seat.

John Petre's West Horndon Hall was demolished in 1763 and replaced by the current Thorndon Hall, a mile or so to the north. Only two pictures of the old West Horndon Hall are known - one on a map by John Walker dating from 1598 and another by an artist who accompanied Grand Duke Cosmo III of Tuscany on his visit to the building in 1669. An archæological dig at the site in the late-1950s and early-1960s revealed traces of the building's foundations and gave archæologists a good understanding of the evolutionary history of the building from the original brick lodge to the John Petre extensions.

When James I acceded to the throne in 1603 John was created Baron Petre of Writtle in recognition of his services to the monarchy. The designation of Writtle (rather than Ingatestone or West Horndon) for his title is an indication of the comparative importance with which that manor was viewed at this time. Twenty-five years earlier John had faced a legal case over the Writtle lands from a rival claimant who thought he had a better title to the property than the Petres. It was evidently a good claim, since the matter was settled only by Petre buying this rival claimant out.

John's sister, Dorothy, also became an important local land-owner at this time and gave the Petre family at Ingatestone a direct connection with neighbouring Fryerning. In 1607 the Berners family sold some of their land in the village to Sir Nicholas Wadham, a native of Dorset, who had married Dorothy, daughter of Sir William, in 1555. He had earlier bought some land and property at Writtle and was said to be a very hospitable man, his Dorset home being 'like an inn at all times and a court at Christmas'.

Despite this natural hospitality, however, Sir Nicholas did not want all his wealth and property to be inherited by 'his kindred

The tomb of John, 1st Lord Petre

[who] did not care for him' and, because of this, and the fact that the Wadhams did not have any children of their own to look after, they used much of their money to found a college at Oxford for the education of other people's children. The expressed intent and financial backing was provided through Sir Nicholas's will when he died in 1609 and the necessary effort was provided by Dorothy until the couple's dream became reality.

Dorothy may well already have been familiar with the practicalities of college founding because her father had virtually refounded Exeter College with eight endowments of his own some 50 years earlier. Though now 75 years old - and with several of Sir Nicholas's relatives pursuing litigation in order to get their hands on his money - she nevertheless went about the task with enthusiasm and determination and managed to secure the support of King James and several other leading influential men for her campaign.

In 1610 a site for the college was purchased for £860 (site value, plus existing buildings). The foundation stone was laid in July and the new building, to be named Wadham College after its founders, was opened in April 1613. Dorothy had the right of appointment of the college warden and of numerous other members of staff and scholars. Surviving letters show that she took a very active interest in the day-to-day running of the college.

Apart from the money bequeathed by her husband, Dorothy herself also provided some additional funding, plus books for the college library, as well as over half the revenue of her Essex lands. Much of this land passed into college ownership on her death in 1619, when Wadham College also became the patron of the living of Fryerning parish, giving it the responsibility of nominating the rector when the post became vacant. A lavish memorial service was held at the college in gratitude for all the work that Dorothy and Sir Nicholas had done for its founding.

When John Petre died in 1613 he was succeeded by his son, William (1575-1637), as the 2nd Baron Petre. In recognition of his father's achievements, William built a new north chapel at Ingatestone church and commissioned a massive memorial to him.

This memorial is probably still the building's greatest monumental treasure despite currently being in need of some expensive restoration work. The memorial features a long elegy championing the virtues of John Petre as a `great and noble man'. "The affection of the people," claims the elegy, "and friendship of the nobility, he received rather than courted, choosing as his friends always those of highest character, not always those of highest birth, and neither feared nor earned the wrath of those in power, having a strength and a certain heroic vigour of mind... dutiful to God, loyal to his Sovereign, he displayed the greatest compassion towards the poor and spent his youth in honest pursuits and in none that did not become a nobleman..."

Many members of the Petre family were destined to be buried beneath the floor of both this new chapel and the older south chapel. Coffins were stacked on ledges on either side. In the mid-19th century, when the chapels were no longer used for such burials, part of the floor of the north chapel subsided and a section of a monk's cowl and some hair were found there.

Towards the end of Elizabeth's reign the Petre family commissioned several maps of their estates from the renowned father-and-son map-making team from Hanningfield - John Walker senior and John Walker junior. The Walkers were commissioned by Essex landowners to draw maps of various parts of the county from about 1584 to 1616. Their work for the Petres included maps of West Horndon Hall (1598), Ingatestone High Street (1601) and Ingatestone Hall (1605). The map of the High Street is particularly celebrated since it shows detailed rows of timber-framed, plastered buildings and gives a very good guide to how the village looked at the turn of the 16th/17th century. Long-vanished public houses are just one of the many fascinating features to be shown, though the *Bell* inn, then apparently a private house, is one building shown then that survives to this day.

Ingatestone village was quite a prosperous one at this stage, even having its own annual fair. This was originally held on 20th November - the feast day of St Edmund - but in later years, following the introduction of the Gregorian calendar, it was moved to 30th of November and then the 1st of December. The highway upon which the village had grown up and the fair had been established was becoming increasingly important and a number of measures were introduced to bring improvements to this increasingly popular roadway.

In Sir William Petre's day the maintenance of the highway had been a somewhat haphazard affair. In the early days of highway maintenance each stretch of road was the responsibility of the landowner whose property bordered the road and, needless to say, not all of them took this responsibility seriously. Journeys could be rough and uncomfortable, even for visiting monarchs!

The Highways Act of 1555, however, removed the responsibility for the upkeep of roads from landowners whose property bordered the road and introduced the concept of all local people being responsible for the upkeep of local roads. In practice this meant that each parish had to elect two highway surveyors to monitor the condition of local roads and every family had either to pay for labourers to carry out any necessary repairs or actually do the work themselves to ensure that highways were kept in good repair. On a much-used road like that at Ingatestone, where wheeled vehicles were increasingly coming into use, this must have been quite a burdensome task.

The Petre family had their own coach, of course, but most of their less well-off neighbours in the village probably still travelled either on horseback or, more likely, on foot. In 1556 Sir William Petre had paid 13s 4d to examine a coach of revolutionary new design and had evidently acquired either that very vehicle or one like it by 1560. The appeal of this vehicle was partly in the fact that the roof and body were joined together as one (this was not the norm before then) and partly that the body of the coach rested on leather straps rather than being joined to the axles, an arrangement which presumably made travelling a more comfortable affair.

By 1577, lavish improvements to the interior of coaches were all the rage, apparently for the purpose of deluding oneself that the

TO
LONDON
23
Ingatstone

Chelmsford Brentwood
6   5

Ingatestone mile post - a day's horse-ride from London

journey was not as uncomfortable as it was. John Petre paid £30 7s 1d for a coach whose interior was `lined with forty yards of Bruges satin and was provided with green taffeta sarsenet net curtains'.

The situation of Ingatestone at a convenient day's travelling distance from London had always made it an obvious choice as a stopping-off point for travellers. In later years, when regular postal and carrier services started up and began to develop beyond all expectations, it became, not surprisingly, a `staging post' for through-services. The fact that there were later to be so many inns in Ingatestone - 27 at one count - no doubt owed much to the demands of this new through-trade: public houses provided shelter and refreshment for riders and, just as importantly, a change of horses for those bound either for Colchester or for the Capital.

The bustling highway saw one final memorable event as the 16th century drew to a close - the visit in 1599 of the actor, Will Kemp, a contemporary of Shakespeare, who had appeared in many of the playwright's works. Kemp, who was accompanied by the musician, Tom Slye, on fife and tabor, had accepted a bet to morris-dance all the way from London to Norwich, with a view both to making a bit of money and also giving himself some welcome publicity. He chose Ingatestone as one of his stopping points and the trip took him almost four weeks (nine days of actual dancing). His record of the journey gives a good insight into the condition of the road at the time - at Chelmsford he danced waist-deep into a pothole!

THE 17TH CENTURY

As the first decade of the 17th century opened and progressed, the incumbency at Ingatestone church passed into the hands of Nicholas Cliff(e) (rector 1609-19). Cliff was a great friend of the Petre family and was defended by them against criticism for his supposed Catholic leanings. He had relatives of his own in the village and he also held the living at West Horndon, another locality with Petre family connections. And as if two parishes were not enough, he later had the living of West Tilbury as well. It is from Cliff's time at Ingatestone that the oldest of the church's six surviving bells dates (1610) - a rare example of the work of the craftsman, Peter Hawkes.

At neighbouring Fryerning there was a quick turnover of rectors after the long incumbency of William Owen. In 1620 alone, the year of Owen's death, there were three new rectors. The first of these, Robert Nutter, was appointed by Peter Whetcom(be), a trustee of the Wadhams', who was also grandson to old Sir William Petre's sister. The second was Thomas Basill, who was the first rector at Fryerning to be appointed by Wadham College, which had acquired the right of appointment from Nicholas and Dorothy Wadham the previous year. The third, William Smith, had already been appointed as successor to Nicholas Cliff at Ingatestone one year earlier and he proceeded to run the two churches simultaneously until 1630, at which time he resigned to take up the Vice Chancellorship of the University of Oxford.

Smith was one of many West Country men to be appointed to Ingatestone's and Fryerning's churches and he also had a strong connection with Wadham College, where he was already Warden. He may have had a curate operating on his behalf in the locality for much of his incumbency since he appears to have been busy at the college for much of this period, presumably preparing for his Vice Chancellorship.

It is from Smith's time as incumbent at Ingatestone that dates another impressive monument inside the parish church - a portrait bust of Captain John Troughton dating from 1621, which is on the east wall of the south aisle. This monument is apparently the work of Epiphaneus Evesham, who designed a number of church memorials in Essex, including the impressive one to Lord Rich in Felsted church.

Captain Troughton was a one-time employee of the Petre family, who, with his brother, Charles, had come to Ingatestone from their native York, where their father was a baker, and had risen through the ranks of the Petre household at West Horndon. Charles became a departmental head, responsible for the horses, and then went into farming; John became Lady Petre's page.

He left the Petres' service sometime between 1581 and 1586 and was at sea by 1590. In that year he was involved in the capture of a Portuguese ship, *Spiritus Sanctus*, which had been bound for the East Indies. By 1600 he was captaining the ship *Lioness* in naval battles against Spain and Portugal.

In 1601 he became involved in a scandal, when confiscating the cargo of the Portuguese ship, *White Greyhound*. The incident led to a protracted court case when Troughton was sued by the ship's owner on the grounds that it was not strictly an enemy ship and so not all the cargo could be legitimately regarded as booty. The case was not concluded until 1605, when Troughton was initially fined but subsequently discharged. He evidently felt guilty enough about the incident, however, to leave some money in his will to the children of the Lisbon merchant whose cargo he had confiscated!

On the same wall in the church, just a few feet north of the bust of Troughton, is yet another effigy monument to the Petre family of the era - a kneeling statue of Robert Petre, Sir William's youngest brother (1593). The inscription records that he "lived and died a faithful officer to the most famous Queen Elizabeth".

The 2nd Lord Petre, Sir William's grandson, was succeeded by his own son, Robert (1599-1638), as 3rd Lord Petre, and he by his son, William (1627-1683), as 4th Lord Petre.

The 4th Lord Petre achieved some fame nationally, though principally for the wrong reasons. He lived through a turbulent period in English history, when the Civil War was raging between King Charles I and Parliament, and was reported, apparently incorrectly, as having supported the Royalist cause at Edgehill. Ingatestone Hall was searched by Commonwealth soldiers. He was fined and imprisoned for his alleged 'crimes'. Some of the Petres' property was confiscated, being returned only at the Restoration of the Monarchy.

In 1678 he was accused by Titus Oates of being involved with the so-called Popish Plot, a charge no doubt levied due to his widely known Catholic beliefs. Ingatestone Hall was again searched and Petre was imprisoned in the Tower of London. He died there five years later, despite continuing appeals to Charles II for recognition of his innocence. His last letter to the King claimed that he was the victim of 'a false and injurious calumny'. "With my last breath," he wrote, "I beg of God to defend your Majesty from all your enemies and to forgive those who by their perjuries have endeavoured to make me appear to be one." Unfortunately, it was all to no avail.

The 4th Lord's cause for recognition as a respectable man was apparently not helped by his first wife, who was notorious for spending money and not repaying any that she had borrowed and who was noted by the diarist Samuel Pepys as being 'lewd', 'drunken' and 'an impudent jade'.

William was succeeded by his brothers, John (1629-1684) and Thomas (1633-1706), as 5th and 6th Lords Petre. Their cousin, Father Edward Petre, a descendant of the 1st Lord's third son, Thomas, was confessor to James II. He came from the Cranham line of the Petre family, founded by this latter Thomas, and, in common with many of his clergyman contemporaries, met with varying degrees of support and persecution, depending on which way the wind was blowing at the time. Father Edward may well have lived at Ingatestone Hall for a time before James II's accession.

Apart from its ultimately tragic effects on the life of the 4th Lord Petre, the Civil War had some minor effects on Ingatestone village as a whole. In 1648 Royalist troops were pursued by the Parliamentarians from Stratford to Colchester, where a long and unpleasant siege within the town walls was destined to take place. Fortunately, however, little of the criminal damage that was wrought upon other villages in the county during this period appears to have occurred at either Ingatestone or Fryerning. What is unfortunate, though, is that the reactions of Ingatestone people to the passage of troops through the village have not been recorded for posterity. No doubt there would have been many a tale to tell.

One thing that is recorded from this era - in the earliest parish registers, which date from this time (or even earlier in Ingatestone's case) - is the names of several old local families, many of which will still be familiar to current Ingatestone and Fryerning residents. These include Bangs, Beard, Binder, Body, Brasier, Chipperfield, Garfoot, Gilman, Glasscock, Greene, Humfrey, Marsh, Middleton, Nash, Parmenter, Petre, Pomfrey, Pond, Ramm, Shuttleworth, Tabor and Witham. And many others.

A knock-on effect of the Civil War that did have repercussions for one local man was the policy of removing certain rectors from their livings because they happened to hold beliefs that were not tolerated by those in power at the time. At Fryerning, the Royalist rector William Peyton - who had replaced the short-lived but equally Royalist George Gillingham in 1632 - was thus removed in 1644 and replaced by two successive 'Commonwealth intruders' (as rectors during this period came to be known). These 'intruders' - William Beard and Samuel Smith - were said to have served the community 'without mission or jurisdiction' until 1657.

Conversely, however, at Ingatestone, rector John Willis held staunch Commonwealth views and kept his incumbency for upwards of thirty years. His removal, for non-conformity, came in 1662 following the Restoration of the Monarchy. The church's ancient hourglass stand, on the north wall of the nave, is almost certainly a surviving symbol of Willis's time at Ingatestone.

Rector Willis was an acquaintance of rector William Smith, his immediate predecessor at Ingatestone, and may well have acquired the living as a result of Smith's recommendations. His time at Ingatestone, to whence he came from Hockley, must have been dominated by the arguments raging at a national level between the King and Parliament. The land in the parish would have been included in the parcel of land south of the Bishop's Stortford-Colchester road that was declared forest for the King in 1635. This could not have been a popular measure with local landowners. Then there would have been the `ship money' dispute - a request from Charles I for hitherto exempt inland parishes, such as Ingatestone and Fryerning, to provide money for the construction of ships for the Navy. This, too, could not have been popular with local people.

On a more parochial note, one interesting local dispute from Willis's time - a complaint against William Brett for allowing his cows to stray from the field next to the church into the churchyard - serves as a useful reminder that what is now the playing field Recreation Ground was formerly a field for the pasturing of cattle and sheep. John White and John Body were similarly taken to task for allowing hogs to enter and disturb the churchyard during this period.

By the time of Willis's removal, neighbouring Fryerning was in the hands of rector John Peake, son of a Chelmsford headmaster, who was prepared to conform to the new ways of post-Restoration church business and was consequently able to stay in office and bring a period of stability to the village with a lengthy incumbency of his own of over thirty years. He was only in his late twenties when he took up the post.

Peake's personal life was unfortunately marred by the tragic death of his young daughter, Elizabeth, in 1665 - the year of the great plague. It is not certain that Elizabeth died of this disease, but others in the neighbourhood certainly did. The Pest Field in Stock Lane may well have been pressed into service again for the burial of plague victims and the deceased almost certainly included travellers who were passing through Ingatestone in their attempts to escape the epidemic which was raging in London.

There is no doubt that Ingatestone was increasingly becoming an important stopping-off point for travellers at this time. In 1635 Charles I had authorised the use of his Royal Mail coach for the transportation of public letters and, not surprisingly, this led to an increase in the number of letters being sent. The job of post-boy, someone who carried letters on behalf of the public, sprang up. Ingatestone was an obvious choice as a staging post in this new mail system (from whence the word `post' in a mail context comes) because it was on the main road and had a number of inns where horses could be changed and letters could be deposited and collected.

In 1636 the inns were sufficient in number to be a major feature of the town, which was described at the time as being `a good town for market and excellent neat entertainment for travellers'. A number of innkeepers had also apparently taken to brewing their own beer at this time and in 1637 71 Essex brewers lodged a complaint that the innkeepers should be receiving their supplies from established brewers rather than making it themselves. As there was a large number of inns in Ingatestone and Fryerning this may well have had a big effect on the competition.

In 1638 Charles I had himself passed through the village on his way to meet Mary Medici - the dowager Queen of France and the mother of his wife, Queen Henrietta Maria - at Chelmsford. Medici had arrived at Harwich and the road from there to London was filled with travellers bringing news of her arrival and also of the expected arrival of the King.

Two other notable travellers who passed through Ingatestone at this time were the contemporary diarists Samuel Pepys and John Evelyn. Pepys was Member of Parliament for Harwich, where he also had naval responsibilities, and he had therefore of necessity to pass along the highway through the village on the way from his constituency to the Capital. Evelyn passed through Ingatestone at least twice - when travelling from Colchester to Greenwich in 1656 and from London to Cressing Temple in 1658 - and may well have stayed in the village. He also had first-hand contact with William, 4th Lord Petre, in 1679 when Petre and Pepys were imprisoned together in the Tower of London and he recorded the meeting in his diary. "I dined," he wrote, "with Mr Pepys in the Tower, he having been committed by the House of Commons for misdemeanours in the Admiralty when he was Secretary: I believe he was unjustly charged. Here I saluted my Lords Stafford and Petre, who were committed for the Popish Plot."

Towards the end of the 17th century Ingatestone church was under the guidance of rector John Ewer, whose 54-year incumbency (1662-1716) is one of the longest in the parish's history.

Ewer came to Ingatestone after brief state service in the Navy and a curacy at Sawbridgeworth in Hertfordshire. His habit of keeping the registers meticulously at Ingatestone, which received much praise from Wilde, has enabled historians to get a detailed insight into the work of the church and the nature of the community at Ingatestone in the late 17th century. Details of plague and smallpox victims, inns and tradesmen, clergymen and clerks, plus pew descriptions and places of burial, are all recorded. The deaths of ruling monarchs and members of the Petre family are all noted in the registers and news is even given of major events such as the Great Fire of London in 1666, details of which were no doubt imparted to the rector by travellers along the highway through the village who were fleeing the city to escape the disaster. The passing of James II's coronation is recorded, as are countless details of individuals in the locality including a birth in the church porch and, unfortunately, some of the deaths of the rector's own children. In 1692 King William and Queen Mary visited Ingatestone, probably dining at one of the inns on the main road. Unfortunately, however, and perhaps rather curiously when one considers his usual penchant for the recording of historical detail, not even rector Ewer tells us where exactly the meal took place.

Rector Ewer died in 1716, but his exact burial place, though no doubt at Ingatestone, is regrettably uncertain - a sad irony, when one considers the meticulous detail with which he recorded the major events in the lives of so many others.

While Ingatestone was in the capable hands of John Ewer, Fryerning was in the equally safe care of the rector Robert D'Oyley successor to John Peake and, like Peake, only in his late-twenties when he arrived. Over the years, though, D'Oyley was to become a very learned and active individual who was to spend 45 years as rector of Fryerning (1688-1733). What is said to be the oldest tombstone in the churchyard - that of John Harris (1693) - dates from the time of his tenure.

D'Oyley's long incumbency - the longest traceable in Fryerning's history - was not, however, without its difficulties.

Fryerning church (from long path)

THE 18TH CENTURY

As the new century developed, Fryerning rector Robert D'Oyley began to find his sympathies at odds with the changing reigning houses. He had been sympathetic to the Stuarts, sharing their belief in the divine right of kings, and had even been chaplain to the pro-Stuart Lady Elizabeth Hastings, daughter of the seventh Earl of Huntingdon. But the advent of the Hanoverian monarchy, whose first king, George I, brought new views with him when crowned in 1714, was not so much to his liking.

Locally, too, D'Oyley was in some bother. In 1725 he had an altercation with the church's bell-ringers, led by William Flint, who had managed to get into the locked building one Sunday morning at 6 a.m. to ring the bells - despite express orders from the rector to the contrary. D'Oyley made an indignant note about the incident in the church register, recording that 'six or seven fellows' were involved, with Flint, a local publican, 'having in an undue manner possessed himself of the keys of the church'. During this episode a hole was made in the north wall of the church - presumably for the trapped ringers to escape through, since they somehow came to be locked inside the building - but unfortunately the final outcome of the two sides' exchanges is unknown.

D'Oyley met his biggest match, however, in the person of Charles Hornby, who moved to the area late in the rector's incumbency and bought a lot of property in Fryerning, including Huskards and some land at Furze Hall. Hornby was a lawyer, a scholastic equal to the rector and a lover of controversy. Reverend D'Oyley had for some time been failing to fulfil his obligations to pay various local rates (the Churchwarden's Rate, Constable's Rate, Highway Rate, Maimed Soldiers' Rate and Poor Rate) and had apparently been collecting 'unjust tithes'. Hornby wasted no time in bringing this to the notice of the rector's parishioners.

Not one to be shy of the limelight, Hornby began his attack with a pamphlet entitled *A Letter to the Rector of Fryerning on his refusing to pay his rates to the parish assessments.* This 'letter' included on its title page the Biblical quotation "Thou which teachest another, teachest thou not thyself?" and developed from being a wide-ranging criticism of the conduct of clergymen in general into a personal attack on the rector and his methods. All this must have made for interesting times in the village!

Robert D'Oyley died in 1733, leaving a large sum of money to a whole range of worthy causes and a big library of books, with instructions for them to be sold in London. He had earlier given a flagon as a gift to the church as part of its Communion plate. He was buried in his home village of Southrop in Gloucestershire. Charles Hornby died in 1742 and was buried with his wife Alice (d.1736) in the chancel of Fryerning church. He, too, left money to the poor. Rectors at Fryerning from D'Oyley's time until long after were served as parish clerk by members of the Cable family for a total of almost 150 years.

From 1733 to 1753 the incumbency of Fryerning church was in the hands of John Leaver, who had previously been at Hockley. Leaver was succeeded by John Blake, who was to spend 30 years as rector, though by no means all of them in residency in the parish.

Like some of his predecessors, Blake also held the living of Eastwood simultaneously with that of Fryerning and was often absent from the parish. During these absences, at both Eastwood and, especially, Staple Fitzpaine in Somerset (where he also had connections), much of the administration work at Fryerning was handled by the Ingatestone rector, Pierce Lloyd, who made important observations on the organisation of the two neighbouring Ingatestone and Fryerning parishes at the time. He reported, for example, that 'the parish of Fryerning is so intermixt with Ingatestone that the separate extent of it cannot be easily determined'. A reference, no doubt, to the curious interlinked nature of the two parish boundaries. There were 185 houses in Fryerning at the time. Blake died in 1782 and was buried at Staple Fitzpaine.

At Ingatestone the long-serving rector, John Ewer, had been succeeded by Thomas Ralph, who had a long incumbency of his own, lasting 39 years (1716-1755). Ralph had been curate at Ingatestone during Ewer's declining years of ill-health, having previously also worked at Rawreth.

His most significant contribution on a national scale seems to have been his subscription to the plot to reinstate a Stuart Pretender to the throne in 1745. Upon his death ten years later, he left charitable donations and extensive book collections to both places where he had held the incumbency.

Rector Pierce Lloyd, Ingatestone incumbent from 1755 to 1770, was the third successive rector to keep good records of the village. With the long incumbencies of Ewer and Ralph before him, this meant that there were only three rectors at Ingatestone in over a century. Lloyd remained resident at Ingatestone throughout his incumbency and took an active interest in the life of the village.

It was around this period, too, that Ingatestone parish was `consolidated with [that of] Buttsbury', putting the Ingatestone rector in charge of both churches and giving the two villages closer community ties - an arrangement which continues to this day.

A memorial stone to Reverend Lloyd, situated on the floor of the chancel in Ingatestone church, recalls that `like his sacred Lord, he spent his Days/In Acts of Goodness: earning Virtuous Praise'.

In the Petre family the 7th Lord, Robert (1689-1713), had become head of the family from 1706 onwards - the same year in which a national `Survey of Papists' had reported that there were 116 `papists' living in Ingatestone, Fryerning and the surrounding area. The 7th Lord's most notable act was not, however, religious, but the cutting of a lock of hair from the head of his cousin, Arabella Fermor - an incident which led Alexander Pope, a friend of the family, to write *The Rape of the Lock* (1712). The poem was apparently written in an attempt to diffuse the situation, since the incident had supposedly upset several members of the Petre and Fermor families, but it actually served to prolong the discussion about it as some liked the poem and some did not!

Robert was succeeded by his son, also Robert (1713-1742), as 8th Lord Petre in 1713. This Robert was an expert horticulturalist and

49

botanist and developed the gardens of West Horndon (Thorndon) Hall beyond all expectations, introducing several new and unusual species of plant. He had the largest hothouses in the world and a magnificent pine grove. He successfully transplanted mature elm trees and introduced several new water features. He kept rare plants and tropical fruits and laid out the gardens with avenues of trees and eye-catching features such as a cedar of Lebanon planted atop a specially-made hill.

Apart from the attention he gave to the grounds, he also made some alterations to the Hall itself at this time. He commissioned the architect Giacomo Leoni to draw some plans for him for the remodelling of the Hall in 1733 and some of the work suggested by Leoni was carried out between 1734 and 1742. This included the introduction of more symmetry and a more Palladian appearance and feel to the mansion. There was a new central portico and, in 1739, a new chapel was opened by Bishop Benjamin Petre, a relative, who consecrated the altar and said mass during two `exceeding cold' days in November.

The 8th Lord was an acquaintance of the well-known botanist, Peter Collinson, who described his companion's early death in 1742, at the age of just 29, as "the greatest loss that botany or gardening ever felt in this country". The 8th Lord was skilled, he wrote, "in all liberal arts, particularly architecture, statuary, planning and designing, planting and embellishing his large park and gardens... [He had] a great ardour for every branch of Botanic Science - whoever sees his vast plantations and his catalogue will not doubt it". Some remnants of the 8th Lord's work are still visible in the landscape around what is now Thorndon Country Park, but unfortunately many of the special features which he introduced have long-since disappeared.

During the first half of the 18th century, when D'Oyley, Lloyd and the 8th Lord Petre were going about their business, significant attention was also being paid to the local infrastructure. Continuing improvements were being made to the roads around Ingatestone and in 1725 a Turnpike Act was passed to cover the road through the village from Shenfield to Chelmsford. This new legislation, much in abundance at this period, meant that travellers using the road now had to pay a toll to do so. Charges levied at the turnpike paid for the upkeep of the road, which was administered in the locality by the Essex Turnpikes Trust.

The work being done on the road surfaces at this time did not, however, meet with the full approval of all travellers on the road. The Earl of Oxford, for example, had to make an unplanned visit to Ingatestone Hall in 1737 while waiting for the wheels of his coach to be repaired in the village after they had unexpectedly caught fire. And in 1769 the *Ipswich Journal* reported on the inquest into the death of Richard Aimes that `it appeared the deceased was thrown from his horse, a little this side of Ingatestone, into a ditch and was suffocated by mud and filth'.

Another visitor to Ingatestone during this period was the writer, Daniel Defoe. In his *Tour Through The Whole Island of Great Britain* (published in three volumes 1724-6), he made two references to the village, covering the church, the Hall and the rôle of the local community in supplying provisions for Londoners. "In the parish church of this town," he wrote, "are to be seen the ancient monuments of the noble family of Petre; whose seat and large estate lie in the neighbourhood; and whose whole family, by a constant series of beneficent actions to the poor, and bounty upon all charitable occasions, have gained an affectionate esteem through all that part of the country." Ingatestone, Chelmsford and Brentwood were described as "large thoroughfare towns, full of good inns, and chiefly maintained by the excessive multitude of carriers and passengers, which are constantly passing this way to London, with droves of cattle, provisions and manufactures..."

Many of the oldest surviving buildings in Ingatestone High Street date from the 1720s and 1730s - suggesting that this was a period of great prosperity for the village.

Dr Samuel Johnson also passed through the village when travelling to Harwich with his biographer, James Boswell, in August 1763. Boswell records that their coach stopped for lunch somewhere between London and Colchester (where they were staying the night), where they dined at an inn. This must surely have been at either Ingatestone or Chelmsford.

In the Petre family, the 8th Lord's son, yet another Robert (1742-1801), succeeded as 9th Lord Petre on his father's death. The 9th Lord did not share his father's passion for botany and nor was he keen on inheriting a, by then, very ancient and unfashionable building, so he instead set to work on commissioning the architect James Paine to design a completely new Thorndon Hall a mile or so to the north. Work began on this building in 1764 and continued until 1770. The finished product, whose grand central columns may well have originally been intended for the 8th Lord's scheme for the remodelling of the old hall, was a much more Palladian and symmetrical construction than the building which it replaced. The old hall, dating back from before the 1st Lord (John) Petre's time and which may well not have been occupied by the family after the 8th Lord's death, was demolished, and the 9th Lord moved his entourage into the new Georgian mansion which survives today on the edge of Thorndon Park Golf Club.

The 9th Lord was heavily involved in local business, giving his backing to the case for a new Chelmer & Blackwater canal, which was planned to help local trade. He was also a leading supporter of Catholic emancipation, though this, surprisingly, did not exclude him from courtly circles and he managed somehow to maintain close connections with George III, who stayed at Thorndon Hall in October 1778 when on a visit to review his armies with Lord Amherst at Warley. The 9th Lord's diary of the event makes interesting reading, with minute detail of the preparations that were made in the weeks leading up to the visit. These included the purchase of new upholstery, gold-plated candlesticks and cutlery and the introduction of numerous innovative culinary preparations. Much of the crockery to be used to cater for the large entourage which would accompany the King was borrowed from other Essex families, including the Mildmays and the Waldegraves. Up to 100 cooks and other workers swarmed around the house in the fortnight or so before the King's arrival, making sure that everything was how it should be for the visit of a member of the Royal Family.

The King and Queen arrived at Thorndon on 19th October. The 9th Lord's diary records the detail. "At ten minutes after three behold in the Avenue the finest sight of the kind I ever saw. The sun bright out, the army drawn up on each side, innumerable people and the King and Queen appearing with their Equipages, Horse Guards and attendants and numberless horsemen... The Park full of Artillery saluting all the time, the echo of the woods, the shouts of the people, the rapidity with which the King's chaise ran the lawn, in an instant covered with horsemen, the horses panting... made the whole resemble an enchantment... We then had the honour of kissing their Majesties' hands."

This was the second time for Queen Charlotte that she had been the talk of the town in this locality because 17 years earlier she had travelled through Ingatestone when arriving from Hanover in 1761 for her marriage to George III. Like many travellers before and since she had taken the journey from Harwich to London through the village and crowds had lined the streets at various points to see her as she passed.

The King and Queen left Thorndon for Navestock on 21st October 1778. The cost of the two-day visit had been over £1,000 - a very large sum indeed in those days - but it had no doubt helped the 9th Lord's cause.

Lord Petre's Catholic sympathies found an outlet in the growing campaign for Catholic emancipation and his apparently close relationship with the King no doubt enabled him to press the case at the very highest level. His father had permitted the establishment of a Catholic Mission in the chapel at Ingatestone Hall in around 1732 and the 9th Lord had himself experienced Catholic repression at first-hand - an armed force which he had equipped and trained at his own expense for the King's use was not allowed to be commanded by his son, as Catholics could not hold officer ranks. He no doubt intended that others should not find themselves in a similar situation in the future.

The 9th Lord's ardent support for the Catholic cause meant that he was to become a leading member of the so-called First Catholic Committee, which promoted what was to become the Catholic Relief Act of 1778. The Act abolished the system of anti-Catholic informers and the persecution of priests, but did not give Catholics completely equal status with their Protestant counterparts. That was to come with later Committees and statutes, after a long battle for recognition which enraged Protestants and led to serious civil disturbances while the situation was being resolved.

The 9th Lord Petre lived at Ingatestone Hall whilst the new Thorndon Hall was being built and seems to have made several internal and external alterations and extensions there as well. These included the sub-division of certain rooms, the provision of the distinctive one-handed clock over the archway through the outer courtyard buildings and the demolition of the west wing of the main quadrangle, leaving the U-shaped building which is there today.

The 9th Lord Petre died in 1801 and was buried at Ingatestone. He was succeeded by his son, yet another Robert (1763-1809), as 10th Lord Petre. The Petres were served at this time by several members of the Coverdale family, whose tombs can be found in Ingatestone churchyard.

With the Petres in residence at Thorndon and increasing tolerance being shown to Catholics, a small Catholic mission had been formally established in the chapel at Ingatestone Hall c.1732. Notable priests there during this period included Charles Berington (priest 1776-84) who, with two brothers, got into some bother locally for jumping the Mountnessing or Shenfield turnpike gate on horseback instead of stopping to pay the toll. The Beringtons originally came from Stock, but Charles's brother Thomas is buried at Ingatestone.

An important resident at neighbouring Fryerning at this time was Thomas Brand, whose friend, Thomas Hollis (1720-1774), travelled extensively in Italy and elsewhere and brought back with him a collection of ancient busts, marbles, sculptures, statues, vases and jewels and made them available for display throughout Brand's

The Hyde - destroyed by fire, 1965

house, The Hyde - an impressive mansion with landscaped lake-filled grounds which was destroyed by fire in 1965.

The Hyde had been erected, or at least greatly enlarged, in 1719 by Brand's father, Timothy (d.1734), who was the son of a London merchant. There had probably been a house on the site since at least a century earlier - a mention of 'ye Hide Hall' is made in the registers as early as 1624. It was an important enough building to warrant its owner having his own pew in Ingatestone church.

When Hollis died he left much of his property and wealth to Brand, who adopted the name 'Thomas Brand Hollis' in honour of his deceased companion. Foolishly, however, Brand Hollis attempted to increase his status still further by buying a Parliamentary seat - at Hindon in Wiltshire - a practice which was widespread at the time. He was caught, convicted of bribery and corruption, fined and imprisoned. He died at The Hyde in 1804, aged 84, leaving much of his property and his extensive collection to his friend, Reverend Dr John Disney (1746-1816), with whom he shared similar theological and antiquarian views.

Disney came from an old Norman family who took their name from the barony of Isigny in France. Their main place of residence in England was originally Norton Disney in Lincolnshire. Initially an Anglican, Disney renounced that religion in 1782 after developing Unitarian views and became minister of the Essex Street Chapel, near Strand in London. He gave up this post when inheriting The Hyde.

Disney wrote many religious pamphlets and a number of memoirs of acquaintances, including some of Brand Hollis. He died in 1816 and was buried in Fryerning churchyard in the large tomb on the north side of the church. His wife, Jane, who pre-deceased him, is buried south of the church.

Disney was succeeded by his son, also John, whose interest in the inherited collection was much more acute than his father's. John junior spent much time cataloguing his collection and he even added to it himself with a number of Greek vases and relics from Pompeii. He produced a booklet giving full details of the collection and founded the Disney Professorship of Archæology at Cambridge University in 1851. He left his collection to the Fitzwilliam Museum when he died in 1857.

Some other residents of note in the Ingatestone locality during this period were soldiers stationed in the area to guard against expected invasions from France in both the mid-1750s and the late-1790s. During this latter, more worrying, period the French Revolution and the rise of Napoleon were the chief causes for invasion fears.

On a much more local scale, the battles of prizefighters in inns such as the (now-demolished) *Swan* in Ingatestone High Street were taking place at this time, with far less bloody consequences.

The village was flourishing in other respects during this period. The commentary supporting Ogilvy's road map of 1722 describes Ingatestone at this time as being 'a very considerable town'. The November fair on Fairfield (now the Recreation Ground) was going strong and there was a thriving cattle trade. There was a weekly Wednesday market, held in the Market Place in the centre of the village, which was patronised by London dealers and Essex and Suffolk farmers, with many unfortunate beasts being sent off to the London markets at six or seven to a waggon. Welsh farmers were also regular visitors.

At Fryerning, another important development for the agriculture industry was taking place with the rebuilding of the windmill at Mill Green in 1759. It was owned at the time by Lord Petre and was maintained 'by him and his heirs for many decades with the co-operation of the Dearman family, tenant farmers and millers'. The work was carried out by the millwright Robert Barker (d.1784), whose premises included the *Windmill* pub in the Moulsham part of Chelmsford.

For an agricultural community such as Ingatestone this was an important mechanical development. The mill survives to this day, on the left of the road between Fryerning church and the *Cricketers* pub, but it is difficult to see as it is located behind trees on private property.

DANIEL SUTTON

One of the most important Ingatestone residents during the 18th century was 'England's greatest inoculator', Daniel Sutton (1735-1819), who gained great renown for his work in combatting the disease smallpox. This disease, 'the most feared and infectious of all human diseases' since the end of the bubonic plague in 1666, claimed about one in five lives and affected virtually the entire national population at some stage of their lives.

In the first half of the 18th century there were several major epidemics of smallpox throughout the country, which were a great source of fear and concern to everyone. Towns on trade routes, such as those like Ingatestone on the main London-Colchester road, were particularly at risk because of the sheer numbers of people passing through, the attraction of the markets and fairs, the hospitality offered by the inns and the ease of gaining onward transportation. As outbreaks became more frequent and the local economies began to suffer - through loss of trade and the expense of having to pay for care for the sick and burials for the dead - some towns with markets and fairs even banned smallpox victims from entering within their boundaries. It was also commonplace for towns that had suffered outbreaks of the disease to advertise in the local Press that they were 'clear' once the epidemic was over.

In the late 1750s Daniel Sutton's father, Robert, had begun to develop a technique for inoculating people against the disease in the family's native village of Kenton, Suffolk. Inoculation involved 'inserting smallpox bacteria into the human body to give a mild form of the disease in order to produce immunity'. It was widely used in the Middle and Far East and was increasingly being practised by local doctors, but it was also controversial, since smallpox was a deadly disease and the prospect of being deliberately injected with it was not exactly welcomed by large sections of society.

Compared to others who had carried out similar experiments, the method that Robert used was comparatively painless, plus it gave a milder dose of the disease and was less likely to cause permanent disfigurement. But there were still some major objections. Specifically, these were that inoculation was still not yet 100% reliable, that it was expensive to administer and that those who had been inoculated were contagious for a short period and were often thus banned from entering market towns themselves until the period of contagion had abated. Nevertheless, the method gradually gained widespread acceptance and profitable inoculation practices began to spring up all over the place. Robert himself had agents in Suffolk, north Essex and south Norfolk.

Several of Robert's sons followed in his footsteps and Daniel, the second eldest, further improved the method. Then, in 1763, either because of a disagreement with his father or because of a need for independence, Daniel set up in practice on his own. He was 28 at the time. The main differences between his method and his father's were the shortening of the residential period for inoculees (they were usually kept in special inoculation houses away from the main centres of population) and the introduction of a diet of milk, fruit, mercury powder and purging salt. No animal food, spices or fermented liquor were allowed and open air exercise was encouraged.

Though hailing from Suffolk, Daniel chose Ingatestone as the site for his new practice for several reasons. Firstly, it was on a major highway and was a well-known staging post, so there was a potentially large clientele available. Secondly, it was close to London so he could keep in touch with medical developments and also gain the patronage of wealthy City patients, as rich Londoners troubled by smallpox did not have far to come to seek treatment. Thirdly, it was outside the jurisdiction of the College of Physicians, so he could not be debarred from using pioneering - and initially controversial - techniques (though he could still be, and often was, criticised by the College).

Daniel's first advertisement for his Ingatestone business appeared in the *Ipswich Journal* in November 1763, when he claimed to have two inoculating houses available, apparently situated in the Mill Green area of Fryerning. Understandably for the time, however, and despite the location of his houses away from the main road, Daniel's new business generated much opposition from Ingatestone residents. This was a market town with a fair and a prosperous through-trade and the prospect of contagious smallpox inoculees wandering around the town did not go down well with local innkeepers and doctors. Some of the town's more notable inhabitants felt strongly enough about it to use the *Ipswich Journal* to their own ends, stating that they were "determined to give all the opposition thereto that the Law will enable them to do; as infecting a town of so much traffic will be a detriment to the public, and may be easily proved a nuisance".

This approach seriously threatened Sutton's business and it was not until he offered free inoculation to local poor people in 1764, an exercise which was extremely successful, that he began to shake off the initial stigma that his opponents had succeeded in attaching to him. An advertisement in the *Chelmsford Chronicle* in October 1764 confirmed that his business was flourishing - the coaching trade through Ingatestone was showing some signs of decline and consequently his opponents were still vociferous in their campaign against him. By this stage, however, they were resigned to the fact that Sutton was there to stay and were using the *Chronicle* to persuade travellers that they were sufficiently confident in Sutton's business practices to reassure them that Ingatestone was a perfectly safe place to stop.

"No person in the town," they wrote, "has catched the smallpox from Mr Sutton's patients coming into the town... [and] we do further assure the public that every possible precaution is and shall be taken to guard against any danger to travellers who have occasion either to stop or to lodge in the town."

By 1765 Sutton had extended his business into London and the following year he hired Reverend Robert Houlton, a Somerset clergyman, to act as both his campaign publicist and as 'officiating clergyman' to the inoculation houses, of which he now had three in the locality. In 1766 Houlton preached a sermon in defence of inoculation at Ingatestone. This was published, with some additional notes, the following year.

Also in 1766 Sutton gained great public acclaim for his success in treating almost 500 people in Maldon, when a smallpox outbreak there appeared to be on the verge of epidemic proportions, and he received some international recognition when he demonstrated his methods to one of the doctors of the King of Poland.

Between 1765 and 1766 Sutton was at the height of his fame, and from the proceeds of his business successes he was able to buy a house in Fryerning, called Maisonette, which came with 39 acres of land. He may also have owned Brandiston House in Ingatestone High Street (opposite the *Bell*). The precarious nature of the business was also demonstrated at this time, however, when he was blamed, apparently as part of a deliberate slur campaign, for starting an outbreak of smallpox in Chelmsford. He was acquitted after a court appearance on the grounds that virtually every doctor in the town at the time was practising their own method of inoculation and there was no way it could be proved precisely who was responsible.

Sutton's successes took him away from Ingatestone for long periods but he was still returning to Maisonette, which he had once let out on long-term lease, as late as 1792. In 1796 he produced a book called *The Inoculator*, explaining his methods and his views of the medical establishment. He died in London in 1819, aged 83, after a long, eventful and sometimes controversial career in a pioneering medical field.

Though inoculation was later succeeded by vaccination (in which cowpox, rather than smallpox, was injected into patients) as a more effective method of combatting the disease, Daniel Sutton certainly made his mark in the world of medicine and is probably one of the most important unsung heroes of Ingatestone history to date.

J. R. Smith wrote of him that "While there is a temptation to think of Daniel Sutton as not so much a medical practitioner as a very ambitious, energetic and publicity-conscious businessman intent on amassing a fortune, the fact remains that his three years of unrivalled success and supremacy in the mid-1760s marked the beginning of the widespread acceptance and popularity of inoculation in the later 18th century". His obituary in the

Gentleman's Magazine stated that "The benefits which the world has derived from Mr Sutton's practice have been duly appreciated and will cause his name and memory ever to be recollected with respect and honourable distinction".

Brandiston House

INTO THE VICTORIAN ERA

As the 18th century drew to a close, Fryerning church was in the hands of rector Richard Stubbs, who appears to have come from Wadham College, patron of almost all Fryerning rectors from 1620 to the present day (but see later) - at a time when the college was in a brief temporary decline. He was actually appointed, in 1783, by the Bishop of London because the college had been too slow to appoint its own nominated successor to John Blake.

Like many of his predecessors, Stubbs held the living of Eastwood as well as that of Fryerning and also for a short time was responsible for looking after Blackmore as well (though much of the work there was probably handled by his curate, Walter Farrell). Stubbs appears to have been a very busy man, for he is also credited in some quarters with running a small church school and contributing to (or even editing) Peter Muilman's 1770 publication *Gentleman's History of Essex*.

During Stubbs's incumbency at Fryerning, one of the church-wardens, Samuel Perry, planted the Scotch firs which can still be seen in the churchyard today. Another churchwarden, Antony Eglinton, had his name carved on a new bell (1793) which was first hung during Stubbs' time there. One final note of interest for Stubbs' incumbency is that it saw, in 1804, the last burial in wool at Fryerning - a manner of burial made compulsory some 150 years earlier as an attempt to prop up the flagging English cloth trade.

Stubbs died in 1810, when the country's main attentions were turned to the Napoleonic Wars, which occasioned the stationing of many soldiers in and around the Ingatestone area because of the need for forces to be kept close to the coast, the capital and the port of Harwich - any of which might be attacked if Napoleon chose to invade. Stubbs was buried in the chancel of Fryerning church, as a monument inside the building (on the south wall of the nave above the pulpit) records. Walter Farrell, his Blackmore curate, is buried in Fryerning churchyard between the church and the lychgate, though the headstone is now somewhat overgrown with brambles.

At Ingatestone, Pierce Lloyd had been succeeded by two generations of John Lewis's - John Lewis senior (rector 1771-1796) and John Lewis junior (rector 1796-1853). The senior Lewis also held incumbencies at Sandon and Birdbrook and, evidently because of the demands that these made on his time, he became the first non-resident rector at Ingatestone since 1630. The church was looked after by curates, notably John Jenner, who was also a curate at Fryerning for a time. Lewis was buried at Sandon.

John Lewis junior, apparently most likely a nephew of his immediate predecessor, also held livings at Sandon and, later, Rivenhall. His 57-year stint is the longest traceable incumbency at Ingatestone. This Lewis was a more significant figure in the village than his predecessor had been; it was Rivenhall and Sandon during his incumbency that had to make do with curates.

John Lewis junior was remembered by the oldest parishioners in Wilde's day as a `rather short, stout, white-haired old gentleman with a stutter... A good man... but very poor'.

His son, Richard Lewis, was a well-known doctor in the village and was openly proud about the fact that he had not slept one night out of Ingatestone in 50 years.

Members of the Lewis family were buried in a huge brick tomb (11 feet by 19 feet and 8 feet high) on the north side of the church in Ingatestone churchyard. This tomb was so large, according to a mischievous story put about by one wag, that it was once mistaken for the village's infants school! By the 1950s, however, Time had regrettably taken its toll on the structure and it was taken down. Slabs bearing the names of various Lewis family members can still be seen though, lying at ground level on the site of the original structure.

During the incumbency of the first Lewis a new clock was erected at Ingatestone church. Local resident, Thomas Scarfe, installed one in 1780, thought to be a replacement for an earlier clock. Typical of the time, it was weight-driven and hand-wound. It also had no hands or dial on the outside of the tower. All it did was strike the hours. Scarfe was one of two noted Ingatestone clockmakers, the other being William Whichcord, who is buried in Fryerning churchyard.

There is some evidence of a bell foundry being in existence in Ingatestone around this time, too, though little appears to be known about it today. Mrs Wilde suggested several possible sites for the foundry - the south-western end of the village around the maltings (near what is now The Furlongs) and a site in Stock Lane being perhaps the two most likely. Bells at Great Chesterford, Ingrave and South Weald all appear to have been made at Ingatestone.

In 1811 at Fryerning Richard Mitchell succeeded Richard Stubbs as incumbent. The Napoleonic Wars were still raging across the Channel, but the chief topic with which Mitchell was concerned was the seemingly never-ending question of whether Catholics should be emancipated. He thought categorically that they should not be and he even wrote to the Prime Minister, Lord Liverpool (who had his own opinions on the subject), to voice his opposition to proposals to allow Catholics more freedom, apparently unconcerned that the influential and openly Catholic Petre family lived in the next village.

On his death Reverend Mitchell was buried in a high square tomb on the south side of the churchyard, near Curate Farrell. Now this tomb is covered with ivy, making the inscription illegible. He lived long enough, however, to witness the sad torchlit funeral procession one summer evening in 1821 of the body of the late Queen Caroline through Ingatestone on its way from London to Harwich. Caroline was the wife of the unpopular George IV, who had married her solely for her money, to enable him to pay off debts owed to Parliament.

In the Petre family the 10th Lord also passed away, his son, William (1793-1850), becoming the 11th Lord Petre in 1809. William was a great horseman and huntsman, but is perhaps best remembered today for his unyielding stance in negotiations with the Eastern Counties Railway, who wanted to build their line from London to Colchester across the Petre property.

The arrival of the railway at this particular time in the history of the locality was somewhat ironic, since the years 1820-1840 had seen Essex roads in their best light to date. The road through Ingatestone was busy with all kinds of traffic and was usually maintained in good repair. Coaches, carriers' carts, post-chaises, waggons, drovers with their livestock and even little carts drawn by dogs all passed along the highway at this time. In 1833 it took just six-and-a-half hours to travel by coach from Colchester to Piccadilly, for a fare of 12 shillings (six shillings if travelling on the outside). Sir James McAdam, son of the famous John Loudon McAdam, was consulting surveyor to several of the county's turnpike Trusts, including the Essex Trust which looked after the road through Ingatestone.

The village must have seemed very busy at this period. Large numbers of farm animals were still being transported through it on their way to the London markets, though Ingatestone's own Wednesday market had probably gone by the beginning of the 19th century. It had been replaced by a Friday night stop-over as farmers paused in the village before the final leg of their journey to the London markets on Sunday. During this stop-over any lame cattle would be bought-up in the Market Place by Ingatestone butchers. Other animals driven through the town *en masse* included pigs, sheep, geese and turkeys. Cattle were still being driven through the town on Fridays and poultry on Wednesdays into the early years of the 20th century.

There was still a fair on Fairfield in Ingatestone at this time, too, though the date had long-since moved from November 20th to December 1st as a result of the change from the Julian to Gregorian calendar. Some sources cite two annual fairs in the village and neighbouring Fryerning may also have had an occasional fair of its own on the small triangle of village green outside the *Woolpack* public house. Certainly there was a large horse fair on Fairfield at Ingatestone (now the Recreation Ground), which attracted Welsh farmers in particular to the village. The *Star* pub, which backed onto the lane leading up to the fair, made some extra profit by opening a serving hatch onto the lane and cashing in on the thirst of fair traders and visitors alike.

After such a busy and thriving period for transport activity in the village it was with some reluctance that many greeted the arrival of the next major travel improvement - the railway. Its arrival spelt disaster for road traffic throughout the country since it was quicker and usually cheaper to have goods transported by rail. Ingatestone High Street, whose many trade- and travel-related businesses depended heavily for their livelihoods on road traffic, suffered heavily as a result. With reduced carriage trade, there was a correspondingly reduced demand for ancillary trades such as blacksmith, carrier and even publican. Coupled with the decline of the fair and the market, this meant that there was a general reduction in the importance and prosperity of the village at this time. "It was," said Wilde, "like a man in the heyday of life suddenly struck down with a fell and incurable disease."

The railway reached Ingatestone in 1842 and passenger services on the Brentwood-Colchester section of the line began on 29th March 1843. Within five years it could be said of the village that it was once "a great thoroughfare for coaches, waggons, cattle, etc., but the traffic is now mostly drawn into the vortex of the railway". By the end of the century, it could further be said of the place that "it seems to have fallen asleep when the last coach took its last change and never have had the energy to waken again".

The coming of the railway was not, however, all plain sailing for those behind the scheme. The redoubtable 11th Lord Petre objected strongly to the construction of the line across his property at Ingatestone Hall, wanting it to be moved further to the north towards Writtle and Highwood. After protracted "negotiations" between Lord Petre and the railway company permission was at last received to build the line through Ingatestone on payment by the company of a massive financial sum to Lord Petre - £100,000 in compensation, plus £20,000 for the land. Development permissions were also hamstrung by numerous conditions, one of which was that the village railway station had to be built in a style which reflected that of nearby Ingatestone Hall - a decision which, though presumably frustrating to the railway company at the time, has given

Ingatestone Railway Station

their successors a building which is rather more aesthetically pleasing than many of the others on the London-Colchester line.

Apart from the problems experienced by the railway company, Ingatestone people also experienced problems with the railway workers, or `navvies', who were regularly reported to the local police on the grounds of misbehaviour or misconduct. They seemed to wallow in being unruly, stole meat from the butcher's and peas from the fields and were often involved in fights or petty theft, especially on Saturday nights.

Before the arrival of the railway there had been two policemen regularly stationed in Ingatestone - an inspector and a constable. The first full-time regular police force in the county was established in 1840, but there were police officers in the village before that, the earliest traceable being Robert Brock in the 1820s. Policing then had evolved from the mediæval system of parochial policing - regular forces were not introduced anywhere until 1829, when the first full-time uniformed service was set up in London. George Brock, a relative of Robert, was the first stationmaster in the village.

Once the railway had become established, trade in the High Street declined and the police presence was reduced to a single constable. By 1878, however, there were a sergeant and two constables stationed in the village - an arrangement which lasted 100 years. The police station at the time, which was actually the sergeant's house, was at 88 High Street (now Beauty at 88), opposite the *Star* pub. Then, as now, it was divided into two, with a common entrance. The sergeant was Patrick Gallagher, an ex-Ulster Constabulary man, whose house was on the left of the entrance and whose front room was converted into police station offices. The two constables were in lodgings elsewhere in the village.

Locals must have been very relieved once the railway line through Ingatestone was finally completed. Apart from the navvies, they had also had to put up with a temporary station - below the bridge in Stock Lane and accessed by steep stairs from the roadway above - until the current building was completed, several hundred yards south west of the original, in 1846. They also had to get used to some new terminology - the part of the Ingatestone-Hall-bound Old Hall Lane that led from the main road to the station was thenceforth renamed Station Lane.

After their arduous series of negotiations with Lord Petre the railway company must have derived some pleasure from the fact that some of the original Petre almshouses in Stock Lane had to be demolished to make way for the line. They were replaced in 1840 by a new range of almshouses in Ingatestone High Street, initially known as Alms Row, which were built, like the railway station, in a neo-Tudor style that mimicked Ingatestone Hall. The same year also saw the construction of a new Congregational Church in the High Street (replacing the original 1812 chapel which had become too small), but a Catholic church, planned as part of the new almshouses development, was never built - something which was to become a bone of contention amongst Catholics in the village for several years afterwards.

In 1832 Canon George Last had become the new Catholic priest at Ingatestone Hall, which by then was one of seven Catholic missions in Essex. The recent closure of missions at Stock and Pilgrim's Hatch had placed more work at Ingatestone's door and Last worked hard on building up his mission. He fought to ensure that only Catholics were permitted to live in the Petre almshouses as, even during their founder Sir William Petre's time, Anglicans had somehow obtained permission to live there. He also advised on the drawing up of new rules for inhabitation of the almshouses (based on the original ones) and made sure that the names of proposed residents at the almshouses were submitted by himself to Lord Petre for consideration and not by the Anglican rector. Preference was to be given to those living on the Petre estates and the importance of being practising Catholics was stressed to all almshouse candidates. Lord Petre gave a gift of coal to inhabitants every year.

Last also set up a small schoolroom at Ingatestone Hall, before the establishment c.1860 of a new Catholic school at the building known as The Folly in Star Lane (later the site of the doctors, but now [1997] being developed as housing). The school was dedicated

Scott Cottage

to St Erkenwald and St Ethelburga, recalling the village's links with Barking Abbey (which these brother-and-sister saints were said to have founded). The headteacher lived opposite The Folly in the house called St Erkenwald's. The school was closed in the 1920s. Around the turn of the century, the thatched Scott Cottage in Fryerning Lane was also used as a school, a `penny day school' (the cost of a day's tuition) which was almost certainly for Catholics. Berkeley House and the *Crown* pub are also believed to have had penny day schools on the premises at one stage.

Other schools were also appearing in the village at this time. On the site of the current library stood the infants school, built in 1873 as an endowed school in memory of Mrs Quick, a local resident who had been a great protagonist of education for the masses. Mrs Quick and her husband, a retired coffee planter, lived in Trueloves.

Originally built for forty children, the school was later extended. When it was demolished in the 1970s the stone on the front wall bearing the words *In Memoriam* was moved to the new junior school in The Furlongs, where it can still be seen attached to the wall by the entrance. The brick pillars which marked the boundary of the old school are still standing either side of the library building.

A Boys' School was also erected in the village in 1873. Originally called Fryerning School it stood in Fryerning Lane on the Ingatestone side of what is now Steen Close, between the entrance to that road and what is now the Larmar building. As with the infants' school, a plaque from the building was salvaged when the boys' school was demolished and that too can be seen on the front of the junior school in The Furlongs.

Later there was also a Girls' School in Fryerning Lane, on the same site as the current infants school, but close to the road.

In the Petre family the 11th Lord Petre's son, William (1817-1884), became the 12th Lord Petre in 1850 and he began to make his own mark on the county with the construction or extension of religious buildings in several parts of south and west Essex. He was an ardent Catholic and a great benefactor to several Catholic causes, including the constructions of new churches at Brentwood (1861),

Ongar (1869) and Barking (1869). He established a chapel at Thorndon for the burial of Petre family members and burials in the chapels at Ingatestone church were henceforth discontinued.

In 1852 the chapel at Ingatestone Hall was enlarged, but Canon Last's continuing demands for a new and separate Catholic church in the village still fell on deaf ears. After a series of written exchanges, Lord Petre finally told Last that the necessary expense was just too much to ask. "I cannot," he wrote, "consent so to cripple myself for a poor decaying town like Ingatestone." The chapel at Ingatestone Hall was again enlarged in 1863, but the congregation still really wanted their own church so did not contribute a great deal financially to the enlargement works.

It was during the time of the 12th Lord that the first of two priestholes discovered at Ingatestone Hall was found, in 1855. These small hidden rooms, which had been built some 30-40 years after the Hall itself, were used to hide Catholic priests and/or religious artifacts from the Protestant authorities at times of persecution (see earlier chapters). Canon Last was there at the time of the discovery of this first priesthole, when a child's toy fell between two floor-boards on the first floor, necessitating their removal for its return. Underneath the floor a trapdoor was discovered, with a ladder extending down some 12 feet into a tiny hidden room next to the main staircase in the south wing. The bones of a bird, a clay candleholder and a badly decayed yew chest with an inscription to Lady Petre (wife of the family's founder, Sir William) were found there. This room can still be seen, though an additional opening has been formed to make it easier for visitors to view the hiding place.

Perhaps because of the discovery of such secret hiding places as this and the long historical associations of the building, Ingatestone Hall also has its fair share of ghost stories. In 1851 a `presence' was reported in the stair turret in the south west corner of the inner courtyard and there have also been claimed sightings of the ghost of a lady in the Lime Walk, said to be that of Lady Katherine Grey who had been held there under house arrest in Sir William Petre's day.

For local residents, this must have been a fascinating era in which to have lived in Ingatestone. With the market and fair dying and the centuries-old method of road transport giving way to the new-fangled railway, there would have been much more rapid change going on at this time than locals would previously have been used to. Fryerning rector, George Price - who had succeeded rector Mitchell - was so interested in the new railway that he took the opportunity to inspect the new (Stock Lane) railway station by riding his grey pony down the steep steps that led from the road to the platform!

Reverend Price, who was apparently sympathetic to his immediate predecessor's anti-Catholic views, was a noted figure in the locality. A short, stout, white-haired gentleman, he looked after the church building well, receiving compliments for the 'very neat and reputable manner' in which it was kept. On one occasion, when snow was thick on the ground, he held a service at the rectory rather than at the church, so that his parishioners could be in the warm and avoid being frozen to death.

In old age rector Price had to be wheeled into church in a bath-chair but, if infirm of body, he was still at least sound of mind, not tolerating lightly those who failed to show up for services and making examples of them and their families to other worshippers.

Price's one-time curate, Felix Palmer, married the beautiful and locally famous Miss Tindal Atkinson, who was said to have been used as the model for the medal of Britannia struck to commemorate the 1851 Exhibition. Miss Atkinson lived at the Fryerning mansion, Huskards. A near neighbour, a widowed lady at Rectory Cottage, had her own attractions at the time - a group of tame monkeys, whose antics were popular with sightseers.

Rector Price died unmarried in 1861 and was buried in Fryerning churchyard next to his sister and close to Curate Farrell and Reverend Mitchell. The gravestones of both Price and his sister are quite small and bear just the initials and dates of death of the respective individuals. The west window of the church contains Price's coat-of-arms and the coats-of-arms of the Wadham and Petre families. A window in the north wall of the chancel is a memorial to both the rector and his sister. Despite his sometimes rough demeanour, Reverend Price was remembered by his contemporaries as "a good man... all sweet inside".

It was during Price's time that the rector's entitlement to tithe payments was ended nationally, due to the 1836 Tithe Commutation Act. Another important historical ecclesiastical change during Price's incumbency was the 1846 transfer of Ingatestone and Fryerning (and other parts of Essex) from the London Diocese (in which they had been included for some 1200 years) to the Rochester Diocese.

The primary cause of Diocesan rearrangement was the expansion of London into south-west Essex. In population terms this led to an imbalance of numbers in each Diocese and the realignment of those near the Capital swiftly followed. The move to Rochester Diocese was only to be temporary however, since by 1877 London's expansion had continued to such an extent that further re-arrangement was necessary and Ingatestonewas transferred into a new Diocese of St Albans, which had distinct responsibility for the whole of the counties of Essex and Hertfordshire.

Price's successor at Fryerning was Henry Weare Blandford, who initiated a full-scale restoration of the church building (see later chapter), but unfortunately did not live long enough to see the work completed. Blandford was succeeded in turn by Reverend Edward Cockey, formerly Rural Dean of Rochford, who arrived just in time for the post-restoration re-opening ceremony.

Cockey made his name locally by encouraging, perhaps even leading, opposition to a plan by the owner of The Grange to close the local footpath from The Tiles to Beggar Hill. The rector and his parishioners ultimately won the day. Cockey died in 1880 after a 10-year incumbency and was buried beside the south porch of the church. His gravestone can still be seen - right outside the door.

At Ingatestone in the mid-19th century the ageing rector, John Lewis junior, managed to live long enough to witness over half a century's worth of changes at Ingatestone before he eventually died in 1853 at the age of 86. He was succeeded by W. Jenkyn, whose seven-year incumbency seems extremely short when compared with his predecessor's memorable and lengthy stint.

Jenkyn was succeeded - in a `straight-swap deal' - by Lewis Parkin, rector of the parish of South Kelsey, Lincolnshire, whose sick wife had been recommended the need for a warmer climate by her doctors. Parkin remained at Ingatestone until 1886, when ill-health forced him to resign. He died the following year and is commemorated in a window in the south aisle of the church.

Reverend Parkin was a very active rector: he co-founded one of the earliest Working Men's Clubs and Libraries in the village (meetings were originally held in a small room overlooking the churchyard, but later moved to what is now the Community Club) and he also instigated Penny Readings, which were a popular mid-19th century pastime. He was also responsible for the introduction of some new security measures for the Communion plate, which burglars attempted (unsuccessfully) to steal during his incumbency.

Parkin's co-founder of the Working Men's Club in 1862 was Henry Newberry of Docklands (a big house which stood on what is now the Docklands estate), but the current Community Club building was not constructed until 1888. It was paid for by public subscription and built to the designs of the Ingatestone architect George Sherrin. There have been several extensions and alterations to the building since that time.

The parish clerk and sexton for a large part of Parkin's incumbency were, respectively, Joseph Poole and William Asher - two notable characters in the village. Asher had served the Church in Ingatestone so long that he claimed to have `rung in' 50 New Years on the church bells and both men had Christmas dinner with the Parkin family every year for 25 years. Asher in particular seems to have been a bit of a character, well remembered for hitting `inattentive youths' over the head with a long stick during church services and knowing every patch of grass in the churchyard. He would even tell elderly local parishioners where exactly he intended to have them buried when they died!

One of rector Parkin's most significant contributions to life in the village was arguably in his role as a leading and enthusiastic protagonist for the restoration of Ingatestone church - an activity which was to take place in 1866-7. The clergy at Fryerning may well have had their neighbour's bustling achievements in mind when commissioning their own restoration in 1869-70.

Although the construction industry was apparently thriving in Ingatestone and Fryerning, the effects of the agricultural depression of the 1870s were making themselves felt to other members of the community, as they were in other parts of the county. The situation had been worsened by an epidemic amongst cattle in 1866, when hundreds of the creatures had been slaughtered to prevent the spread of disease (perhaps the equivalent of the 1990s BSE scare) and strict transportation measures had been introduced to stop animals being moved around local roads.

The Petre family, with its large estates, suffered particularly badly from this overall dire agricultural situation. As the financial situation grew more perilous, the agent for the 13th Lord Petre, also William (1847-1893), reported in 1893 that "some very strong measures must be brought to bear... if the chief industry of this country is not to be stamped out". These proposed measures would probably have included tariffs against foreign grain. One of the Petres' tenant farmers had given notice to quit because he was not able to compete with the low prices being offered elsewhere and the situation was being worsened, according to Lord Petre's agent, by the family `dealing in a liberal manner with the property' and putting a lot of money into repairing and improving farm buildings.

Despite problems with the agricultural situation, the 13th Lord Petre found time to endow both a library and a school (outside Essex), though these also appear to have met with varying degrees of success. He also wrote several religious pamphlets.

Some major administrative changes were taking place locally at this time, including the long-overdue union of Ingatestone and Fryerning into one civil parish in 1889. No longer would most of Ingatestone High Street be in Fryerning parish! Five years later the 1894 Local Government Act established freely elected parish councils

Workhouse cottages

and one of the local Council's first acts was to purchase some land for allotments the following year. By 1899 it had also made provision for a new cemetery - now the Ingatestone and Fryerning parish burial ground, attached to Fryerning churchyard - on land acquired from Wadham College. The purchase was apparently funded in part by the sale of the workhouse cottages in Ingatestone High Street. The distinctive lychgate in front of Fryerning church was built shortly after the burial ground was acquired.

In 1892, as the century drew to a close, Canon Last, Catholic priest at Ingatestone Hall for some 60 years, passed away. He was buried in the Catholic cemetery at Ingatestone church, his obituary being carried by the *Essex Review*. He sadly did not live long enough to see the construction of a new Catholic church in Ingatestone, but at least he had sown the seeds and it would not be long before such a building would be constructed.

In June 1897 Ingatestone joined the rest of the country in celebrating Queen Victoria's Diamond Jubilee, which took place in hot sunshine on the 22nd of the month. The build up of heat and humidity over the next two days culminated, however, in one of the greatest hailstorms in the country's history and numerous buildings were damaged and trees felled in the Ingatestone and Fryerning area. According to the *Chelmsford Chronicle*, Essex and Bedfordshire were the two main victims of the storm, with thunder and lightning accompanying the hail. Crops were damaged, some animals were killed and people were injured by the sheer force of the hail stones, some of which were almost six inches round and were weighed in the village Post Office at 3½ ounces each.

The storm, travelling south-west to north-east, reached Ingatestone at 2:55 pm. Trees were knocked over at Mill Green, poultry was killed, chimneys were blown down, hay was blown around the lanes and fish were even blown out of local ponds, many landing some distance away in the High Street. Buildings opposite the *Bell*, which faced the oncoming storm, were badly damaged.

Mr Coverdale, Lord Petre's agent at Ingatestone Hall, had first-hand experience of the storm when he and his coachman, Gray, were caught out in it whilst in the vicinity of Furze Hall. "We jumped out of the trap and hastened into the house," he told the *Chelmsford Chronicle*. "First the hail and rain came down vertically and then at a sharp angle. Down came the top of a tree at once... The hailstones riddled the umbrella which I carried. My man's chest and arms looked afterwards as if he had had five minutes with a bruiser. They were discoloured everywhere and full of bumps. The force with which he was struck may be estimated by the fact that although he was wearing a mackintosh, livery coat, sleeved waistcoat and shirt, he is black and blue. His tall hat was dented in. My son got a crack on the head through his hat and there was a bump on his head in a moment as big as an egg."

A relief fund was set up for local farmers because so much destruction had been caused to crops and livestock and shooting was banned during the following season to allow the wild bird population to regain its numbers. It also took several years for local fruit trees to recover their pre-storm potential. The 1897 hailstorm was certainly one to remember.

At the turn of the century, Fryerning was in the hands of the rector Frederick Tufnell, who originated from nearby Springfield and whose father was a curate at neighbouring Ingatestone. Tufnell was noted for his ʽfine presence and beautiful reading', but towards the end of his incumbency his sight began to fail and many of his duties were also fulfilled by curates. The Ingatestone rector, Charles Earle, ultimately took charge of both parishes for a short time, though Tufnell did not actually retire until his wife's death in 1902.

Charles Earle had become Ingatestone rector in February 1886, a few months before his 30th birthday. He hailed from Brentwood and was noted for his ʽunfailing kindness to and knowledge of the people'. His father was doctor to the Petre family.

Earle it was who managed to raise money to fund repairs to Ingatestone church tower, re-hang the bells, smarten up the church interior and provide a new extension in which to house the organ. He also found time to get married - to Ethel Disney, a member of the important local family who lived at The Hyde.

John Disney junior had been succeeded by Edgar Disney (1810-1881), who is commemorated by monuments in Fryerning, Ingatestone and Blackmore churches. He was in turn succeeded by his own son, Colonel Edgar John Disney (father of Ethel), and he by his son, Edgar Norton Disney. Apart from the monuments and memorials at the three churches and the massive tomb on the north side of Fryerning churchyard, the family connection with Ingatestone survives to this day in the street names of Disney Close and Norton Road.

And that was the 19th century - a time of great change in Ingatestone. With the passing of the old century went cockfighting and badger-baiting in the Market Place, the hugely entertaining German bands with their dancing bears (very popular in the High Street in the 1890s) and the cage for drunkards that doubled as a storehouse for coal.

"Poor, quiet, empty little Market Place," lamented Wilde, "with its cattle and cocks gone and even the cage in which drunkards were locked up a thing of the past."

Sign from the old school

CHURCH RESTORATIONS

The Victorians do not always get a good Press when it comes to accounts of their 'improvements' to ecclesiastical buildings, but Ingatestone and Fryerning do not appear to have suffered anywhere near as badly as some other Essex settlements.

The restorations at both Ingatestone and Fryerning churches were carried out by the Chelmsford architect, Frederick Chancellor, and it is presumed that at Ingatestone several features mentioned by the writer and historian, George Buckler, who visited both churches on his travels around the county when researching his book *Twenty-two of the Churches of Essex* (published in 1856), were removed at this time. These included some fine carvings on the ceiling and part of the rood screen. The west gallery at Ingatestone was also removed, to open up a view of the tower, and repairs or improvements were made to the ceilings in the south aisle, chancel and nave. The windows were repaired and the high seats were replaced with stained deal benches. A new stone pulpit was provided and several other internal fittings were either repaired or replaced. The door to the south chapel was closed and virtually all the stained glass in the building was replaced. The main north and south doors had already been blocked up long before the restoration, entry then as now being via the west door through the tower.

It was during the restoration that the mediæval wall paintings (referred to in a previous chapter) were discovered beneath the plaster on the north wall of the nave. The largest of these was a seven feet diameter representation of the Seven Deadly Sins. Copies of the paintings were made by both Chancellor and W. Strutt, but the originals themselves were plastered over again - an agonizing decision following lengthy discussion in the community about the best way to preserve them. Miss Parkin, daughter of the rector, wrote that "after much perplexity my father, the church-wardens and the building committee decided to cover the fresco, and also another small one very faded representing St Christopher, with some sort of

82

preparation which would preserve them safely, in case some future restorer wished to open them up again". There has been recent talk of opening these paintings up again for view, but the cost of this is currently considered to be prohibitive and there is unfortunately no guarantee that the end result would be worth the effort.

Either at this time or leading up to it a three-decker pulpit, a Jacobean font cover and all the ancient box pews were also removed, as were some iron railings in the south chapel (the bases of them are still visible) which were taken out to allow the chapel to be used for services. These alterations included the removal of Squire Disney's personal box pew - seven feet in height - which stood on the north side of the nave below the pulpit.

Petre family burials, which had been carried out below the north and south chapels for centuries, were also discontinued at this time, being largely unnecessary now due to the construction of a new burial chapel at Thorndon Hall. Miss Parkin told Wilde that she remembered going down into the spacious vaults under the south chapel and seeing coffins on ledges on either side. She also remembered the floor of the north chapel subsiding and part of a monk's cowl and some hair being discovered.

The south porch at Ingatestone was removed from the church at around this time, having seen service as both a toolshed and as a home for the Ingatestone fire engine (which was later relocated to a new home in the Market Place). The north porch had itself already been removed by this stage (the north doorway is now blocked up), whilst early in the next century (1905) the church gained a new organ chamber - though unfortunately its red brick design material is not exactly in keeping with that of the rest of the building. It has even been described as `disastrous' in recent church literature.

Many new items were presented by people connected with the building, including a new altar, altar rails and altar-cloth and a new lectern and octagonal stone pulpit.

The re-opening ceremony when restoration was complete attracted a large number of clergymen and laymen from all around the locality. There were at least 20 rectors present from other Essex parishes to hear the Bishop of Rochester preach an appropriate sermon on the text of "And they that shall be of thee shall build" (Isaiah 58.12).

Catering for the ceremony was handled by Mr Ruffell, landlord of the *Bell* in the High Street, who put on a spread at the local school for about a hundred guests 'in a most satisfactory style'.

The total cost of the restoration was £1,600.

The Fryerning restoration, slightly less expensive at around £1,400, was, however, no less extensive. It included: the removal of plaster from the outside walls to expose the Norman building work to view; the repair of brickwork, windows and doors; the removal of a flat plastered ceiling and the construction of new roofs of oak tiles; the renewal of the stone chancel arch; the replacement of much of the interior furnishing, including the old high box pews; the relocation of the organ (itself since replaced); and, as at Ingatestone, the removal of the west gallery to open up the view of the church tower. At the time of the restorations both churches had barrel-organs in use to provide the music, Fryerning's apparently dating from 1826 and Ingatestone's from 1862. Other local churches were, however, still clinging onto the old ways - Margaretting, for example, featured a band playing flutes, clarinets and violins, one member of which was the prominent Ingatestone resident and local postmaster, William Whichcord, who is buried in Fryerning churchyard. Restoration costs were financed in part by a number of local families, including the Disneys, the Kortrights and Mr Hetherington of St Leonard's. Wadham College also made a donation.

With the restoration complete, Fryerning church was reopened in June 1870. Rectors from various local churches were in attendance and the Bishop of Rochester again read the Gospel and preached. Catering for the ceremony - 'an excellent and well-served repast' - was handled by Mr James, the landlord of the old *Spread Eagle*, which was actually in Fryerning parish even though it stood in Ingatestone High Street.

SOME FAMOUS INGATESTONE VICTORIANS

Apart from the extensive church restorations, there was a lot of other building work going on in Ingatestone during the Victorian era. Many of these new buildings - which included several of the village's larger houses that were probably initially intended as country retreats for Londoners - were erected outside the village centre, which itself largely escaped the 'improvements' introduced into many other English towns during the Victorian era.

The principal architect of many of these new residences at Ingatestone was George Sherrin (1843-1909), who in most cases chose an appropriate neo-Tudor design to reflect the architectural history of the village. Sherrin lived in one of his own designs, The Gatehouse, in Station Lane, built in 1884. It was renovated and restored in the 1980s after several years standing derelict.

Sherrin had worked with Frederick Chancellor in Chelmsford before setting up his own London-based practice. His works in the village included (amongst others): The Tiles (later called Barn Mead) and Ard Tully (both 1882); Chantry, Red House, Newlands, Long Holt and Tilehurst (all 1884); Heybridge House (later called Tor Bryan) (1886); the original Working Men's Club (1888); Lightoaks (1892); and Millhurst (1906). He also did designs for the east wing restoration at Thorndon Hall in 1894 after that had been damaged by fire, as well as for numerous other buildings throughout the county. Probably his most famous design, however, is not an Ingatestone building at all - but the dome of the old Kursaal pleasure park in Southend-on-Sea.

Sherrin's son, Francis (Frank) (1879-1953), followed his father into architecture and was responsible for a number of buildings of his own in the village, including the Catholic Church (1931/2), St Ethelburga's (for his mother) (1913) and Fairacres (in Stock Lane, for himself) (c.1920).

The only note of caution for the construction industry in Ingatestone at this time was the 1884 Essex Earthquake, centred on

Wivenhoe, which surprisingly made its effects felt even this far south. The tower of the recently restored Ingatestone church suffered cracks which had to be repaired to prevent further damage, though neighbouring Fryerning church appears to have escaped unscathed.

Another famous Ingatestone resident at this time was Duffield William Coller (1805-1884), a writer and historian who had grown up in the most unusual surroundings. His godmother, Sister Duffield, a refugee Roman Catholic nun, had given him a strict Catholic upbringing at Ingatestone Hall, with the intention of schooling him to become a priest. Sister Duffield died before her plan could be executed, however, and Coller was apprenticed successively to a tailor and then a shoemaker, both times running away from home to escape his allocated trades.

His real love was for the written word and it was only in 1827, when he was apprenticed to a printer in Chelmsford, that he began to find his feet. He had some success with the submission of articles to periodicals and his newly-found close relationship with the printing industry gave him the opportunity to develop his ambitions further. He joined the *Chelmsford Chronicle* and stayed there for 40 years, spending much of that time as editor. He also worked on the *Essex Weekly News*, the *Essex Magazine* and the *Essex Literary Journal*, as writer or editor or both. His principal contribution to Essex history, however, is his *The People's History of Essex* (1858-1861), originally published in instalments and later as a book. It can still be obtained from antiquarian bookshops.

Coller, whose wife's grave can still be seen behind the yew tree by the gate at the eastern end of Fryerning churchyard (along with those of her parents, William and Mary Turnedge), was not the only well-known writer of the day to spend some time in Ingatestone.

The novelist Mary Elizabeth Braddon (1837-1915) stayed for a time at Ingatestone Hall and wrote what was to become one of the best-selling `sensationalist' novels of the period, *Lady Audley's Secret* (1862), as a result of her stay there. Ingatestone Hall is thinly disguised as Audley Court in the novel and several features of the real place appear in the fictional one. These include the well, the one-handed clock and the Lime Walk, where an encounter with a ghost described in the novel is said to have been inspired by a real-life event there in the 18th century when Bishop Benjamin Petre was saved from robbers by the sudden appearance of a big black dog. Copies of a painting of the dog giving details of the event are available from the shop at Ingatestone Hall.

Several elements of the Ingatestone locality such as the location and proximity of the railway station to the Hall - are duplicated in *Lady Audley's Secret*, and Brentwood, Chelmsford and Romford are all mentioned. Such was the success of this and other of her novels that Braddon became known as 'The Queen of the Circulating Libraries'.

She was married to the publisher John Maxwell and somehow managed to combine writing her books and contributing to magazines with raising six children of her own and five from Maxwell's first marriage. Half of *Lady Audley's Secret* is said to have been written in two weeks in a desperate attempt to help alleviate some of the couple's financial pressures. The book has since been turned into a play and a film.

The Gatehouse

And so we come to the 20th century, a period which was destined to feature many changes that Mrs Wilde could never have predicted when she was writing about Ingatestone in 1913. Two World Wars and the massive expansion of the motor car lay around the corner, as, of course, did many other happenings on a purely local scale.

In 1902 Frederick Tufnell was replaced as rector of Fryerning by William House, who came to the village from St Anne's in Limehouse. Evidently an active man, House had been a councillor on the first Stepney Borough Council from 1900-1903 and during his incumbency at Fryerning he oversaw the introduction of a new organ into the church and the construction of a new parish room (which still bears the date - 1904). It was said of the old organ that there had been 'a gradual decay of its powers, equally trying to the organist and congregation, [so] it was decided that it must retire'. Only the organist, Mr P. G. Greenfield, ever succeeded in 'humouring its cranks and weaknesses... to the mingled horror and amusement of the congregation'.

From a historical perspective it is interesting to note that Mr Greenfield's temporary successor as organist, Miss M. Rock, was said by Wilde to have resigned from the post after a very short time in the job because she was 'occupied too much perhaps by her efforts to promote the cause of Woman's Suffrage' - a cause which the fullness of time was to show would go a very long way indeed.

Two other significant local residents at the time were C. J. 'Korty' Kortright and A. P. 'Bunny' Lucas - cricketers together in the Essex county side in the last decade of the 19th century and the first decade of the 20th.

The Kortrights owned a lot of land in the Fryerning area including, at various stages, Maisonette, Mill Green House, St Leonard's, The Hut and Green Street Farm. The family had first settled in the locality around the turn of the 19th century, when C. J. Kortright's great-grandfather, Cornelius, bought Hylands Park, Chelmsford, in 1797. The family's already sizeable fortunes were increased even further when Cornelius's son, Captain William Kortright, married Sarah Coesvelt, daughter of William G. Coesvelt, a painter and collector of pictures who travelled Europe looking for art treasures. Coesvelt and his son, also William G., who predeceased him, are both commemorated by plaques on the north wall of the chancel in Fryerning. The family's accruing wealth meant that by the time it reached C. J. Kortright he could choose to do whatever he wanted in life - and he opted for cricket. He was said to have been rather proud of the fact that he never did a day's work in his life.

Charles Jesse Kortright was born at Furze Hall in Fryerning on 9th January 1871 and was educated at Brentwood and Tonbridge Schools. He played cricket at both, being just 13 when he first got into the Brentwood XI. He made his debut for the Essex county side in 1889 at the age of 28, though Essex itself did not achieve full recognition as a first-class county in the game until 1894.

Said to have been the `fastest bowler of all time', Kortright was the first player to take a wicket for Essex once it had achieved first-class status. Many opposing batsmen faced the bowler with trepidation. Sir Pelham Warner, himself a cricketing legend, remembered later how, when facing Kortright's bowling, "one had to shut one's teeth very tight and remember that for honour's sake one could not run away".

Kortright became captain of Essex in 1903 but, to the surprise of many, he never gained full international honours despite having numerous ardent supporters for the accolade. His style was fast and direct: "he ran 15 yards to the crease, gathered momentum as he ran and delivered from his full height of six feet; he was very fast and very straight". Not for him the swing and spin that other bowlers used. At his peak, between 1895 and 1898, he took 287 wickets for the county, 206 of them without any help from the fielders.

Kortright is remembered amongst other things for keeping his cool in a particularly bad-tempered game against Gloucestershire in 1898 when he was repeatedly turned down for appeals of "Out" against the legendary Dr. W. G. Grace, who refused to walk on several occasions when it looked as if he ought to but no-one had the courage to argue with him. Kortright persisted and eventually made indisputable contact with Grace's wicket, uprooting one of the stumps. Grace, at last, accepted his fate and turned to walk back to the pavilion. As he passed Kortright, the Essex man turned to him and, with heavy irony, addressed him with the comment, "Surely you're not going, Doctor, there's still one stump standing". Grace was said afterwards to have `never been so insulted' in his life. The pair were destined to be reconciled, however, barely a fortnight later when Fate brought them together again on the same side in a Gentleman *v.* Players fixture. They played a valiant last wicket batting partnership and narrowly missed saving the game.

At the end of the 1898 season Kortright was picked to play for the `Rest of England' against the accepted national side which had gone on tour to Australia the previous winter. This was the closest he ever got to playing for the national side, kept out of the team primarily by Surrey fast bowler Tom Richardson, whose county side was rather more established than Essex at the time. A serious back injury kept Kortright out of even the county side in 1899 and when he was finally fit enough to return he had lost a lot of his pace and power. The chance of an England call-up had passed him by.

Though primarily noted for his prowess as a bowler, Kortright had, in 1891, hit 158 v Hampshire (in 1¾ hours during an 8th wicket stand) which was the highest by an Essex player at that time. Evidently something of an all-rounder, his best bowling figures were 8-57 and he also took more than 20 catches in a season on three separate occasions.

Kortright retired from first-class cricket in 1907 and thenceforth spent much of his time as a `country gentleman with all the sporting pursuits that description suggests', punctuated by a brief spell as a special constable in Ingatestone during the 1914-18 war. He was particularly interested in golf, playing both at Chelmsford and Romford before settling at Thorndon Park Golf Club where he was to become a long-serving, well-known and very active member. He also dabbled in the Stock Market and was a keen ornithologist.

Though in retirement from cricket, he was still often interviewed by the media, particularly during the notorious Bodyline Tour when Harold Larwood's bowling feats recalled memories of Kortright's own speed-bowling achievements. He even played the odd game of cricket for local club sides, including Ingatestone, and was playing for Navestock in the early 1930s when he was over 60 years old.

Kortright died on 12th December 1952 when living with his sister Caroline at Brook Street, Brentwood. He was buried in Fryerning churchyard. He was one of the last survivors of the Golden Age of cricket spanning the years from 1890-1914. His obituary in *The Times* stated that "it is one of the remarkable features in the history of cricket that Kortright never once played for England".

Kortright's team-mate, Alfred Perry Lucas - the other famous Essex cricketer of this period - was not, however, a native of the county. Born in London on 20th February 1857, Lucas joined the Essex side in 1889 as a result of his friendship with the Essex team's great mentor, Charles Green. He had already played for both Surrey and Middlesex and had appeared five times for England. He had been coached at Uppingham by H. H. Stephenson, the captain of the first England side to tour Australia, and had shown immense potential as a batsman in hitting over 70 runs in two innings of a Gentlemen of the South v. Players of the North game aged 17. He was captain of Essex in 1894 when the side obtained first-class status and was generally recognised as one of the finest bats-men of his day, the 'great stylist of his generation... a master of both back and forward play' and the best defensive batsman of his era.

Like Kortright, Lucas was involved in the notoriously bad-tempered game against Gloucester in 1898. 'A man of scrupulous honesty' he was declared "Out", caught-behind, on a delivery which he claimed had touched only his shirt and not his bat. This apparently unfair dismissal led to shouts of "cheat" being directed at the Gloucester players by an incensed Essex crowd.

Lucas played his last game for the Essex first team in 1907, by which time he was 50 years old and becoming increasingly deaf. Apart from his batting achievements he had, with Charles Green,

91

done much to ensure that Essex obtained first-class status and he was always regarded as a gentleman of the game.

In retirement Lucas lived for a time at Fryerning rectory and, like Kortright, played the odd game of cricket for the local Ingatestone team. He was a churchwarden at Fryerning for 20 years and there is a plaque in the church to his memory which records that he was "renowned as a cricketer both in England and Australia" and was "a notable example of modesty, piety and blamelessness".

Lucas died on 13th October 1923 and was buried in Fryerning churchyard. Lucas's and Kortright's graves can still be seen, though they are not quite the 22 yards - the length of a cricket pitch - apart that a nice little story about them would have us believe.

While Lucas was a churchwarden at Fryerning another change was made to the local Diocese when in 1914 a new Essex Diocese was created and Ingatestone and Fryerning's 40-year spell under the jurisdiction of St Alban's was brought to an end. The creation of a new Diocese meant that a cathedral church was needed for the county and Fryerning's Reverend House and his fellow incumbents around the Essex parishes were all asked to vote on where they thought the Cathedral should be. There were seven applicants for cathedral church status, the resulting order after voting being Chelmsford, Colchester, West Ham, Woodford, Barking, Waltham Abbey and Thaxted. The ultimate choice of the cathedral church in a town so close to Ingatestone and Fryerning must have led to a great deal of excitement amongst local church-goers at this time.

Reverend House was replaced in 1915 by Sydney Brown, who was also evidently a rather busy man as he employed a curate to take some of his services at Fryerning. He was rector there until 1927 and was also, during his spell in the village, concurrently Chairman of the Diocesan Training Committee (1919-24) and General Secretary for the Central Advisory Council of Training for the Ministry (1924-27). He has been described for his work within the Diocese at this time as 'an outstanding assistant' to the Bishop.

Brown left Fryerning to become vicar of Brentwood, where he stayed until 1935. He then moved on to become Professor of

Hebrew and Exegesis at King's College in the University of London (1935-44) and, after that, spent two-and-a-half years as residential canon of Worcester Cathedral. He died in 1947.

Gordon Hewitt wrote in *A History of the Diocese of Chelmsford* that Reverend Brown was "modest and self-effacing - had he been self-seeking he would have advanced to a leading position in the Church".

At Ingatestone, rector Charles Earle served a long incumbency of over 32 years from 1886 until (officially) the very last day of 1918 (though he had to retire early on the grounds of ill-health in early August). He had originally planned to retire at the end of the Great War and was in any case asked to stay on in name until a successor could be appointed and this was not possible until 1st January 1919.

During Earle's incumbency several changes were made to the structure of Ingatestone church, with the construction of the new organ chamber in 1905, the removal of plaster and whitewashing from some of the columns and arches of the interior and the general cleaning and tidying of the building. During construction of the organ chamber, which was built because members of the congregation had complained that the organ was blocking the view of the chancel, part of the stone from which Ingatestone gets its name was found in the ground by the north wall. This was taken out and placed in the churchyard, where it can now be seen outside the south door.

In 1908 the church tower was restored, primarily because of the damage caused to it by the Essex Earthquake in 1884, and the battlements, buttresses and windows all received some attention.

It was during Earle's incumbency (c.1900) that the old rectory in Stock Lane (now covered by the Fairfield housing estate) was sold by the church authorities into private ownership 'to the lasting regret of by far the greater number of inhabitants'. It was replaced by a modern, if less conveniently situated, rectory in Fryerning Lane (where Rectory Close is now), which had 14 rooms, a small orchard and a large garden. Parts of the grounds of this rectory were later lost with the creation of Willow Green and the Wadham Close old people's bungalows, but it would continue to be home to successive Ingatestone rectors from Earle's day until its demolition in 1989.

Despite his many achievements, Reverend Earle was quoted in the Ingatestone and Fryerning parish magazine towards the end of his period of service as believing that "he has done many things which he ought not to have done and left undone many things which he ought to have done - for all of which he most humbly asks forgiveness". His parishioners evidently considered that he had nevertheless done a great deal, since the then quite respectable sum of £206 was collected for him when he resigned. Sadly, despite his retirement, Reverend Earle's health continued to deteriorate and he died in 1919 when only in his early 60s.

Charles Earle was succeed in 1919 by Robert 'Bobby' Pemberton, who came to Ingatestone from Lyonshall in Herefordshire and was appointed on the recommendation of the then patron, Mr C. E. Arnould. Pemberton had been educated at Oxford and at Wells Theological College and had held numerous other church posts before his appointment. These included the curacies of Forton (Hampshire), Scarborough and Solihull and the vicarial appointments of Sutton Coldfield and Lyonshall. He had, according to the parish magazine editor at the time of his arrival, a depth of experience at working in different parishes 'which his predecessor had always regretted he did not have'.

One of Reverend Pemberton's first tasks, in common with both his own parishioners and countless ordinary people all over the country, was to consider the erection of a suitable memorial to the dead of the First World War.

During Pemberton's incumbency more changes were made to the fabric of Ingatestone church. In 1923 the east window was dedicated to the memory of the one surviving member of a local shooting party who did not die of food poisoning whilst out on the hunt. Five years later, the church clock gained its first external face - that on the west wall of the tower.

Reverend Pemberton is remembered locally as a short man with pince-nez spectacles, who was much looked up to by his parishioners. He was a member of the Chelmsford Rural District Council and evidently played a very active part in village life. He visited the old Boys' School in Fryerning Lane at least once a week to give religious instruction and is still remembered with affection by some ex-pupils. He is also remembered for his Ford Model Y car - one of the first of the £100 vehicles in the village.

The Boys' School at this time had only two rooms. One of these was used as a classroom for pupils younger than eight years old. The other was itself divided into two by a curtain - two forms were taught by one teacher on one side and three other forms were taught by the headmaster on the other. In those days the boys were `kicked out into the world' at just 14 years of age.

The headmaster for much of this period was the highly respected Herbert `Skip' Seymour, after whom the Seymour Field at the Margaretting end of the village is named. In the First World War Seymour had been a fighter pilot and in the Second was a squadron leader. He was not a native of Ingatestone but certainly made his mark in the village, as both headmaster and scoutmaster.

Reverend Pemberton retired in 1940, but sadly did not live long in retirement, dying the following year. The church contains a memorial to him in the form of dedicated oak panelling in the chancel behind the altar. Another lasting memory is Pemberton Avenue, a road originally built as a cul-de-sac in the 1930s, but later extended and named after the rector. Nearby Trimble and Disney Closes had also been started in the 1920s and 1930s. Vera Pemberton, Bobby's daughter, was destined to surpass her father's achievements in the village.

Reverend Pemberton was succeeded by Geoffrey Foulerton, who had been living in the village since April 1940 but who was officially instituted as rector in January 1941. His first impression of Ingatestone was that it was `a friendly place'.

Local schools had `open days' at the rectory at this period, holding gym displays and prize-giving ceremonies. Prizes were collected from the rectory verandah. Miss Pemberton lodged with the Foulertons for a short time, before they left the village and moved north in 1952.

At Fryerning, rector Brown was succeeded in 1927 by Claude Trimble, the last rector to be appointed exclusively by Wadham College, because in 1957, when the next rector was appointed, the parish was joined to Margaretting and the exclusive right of appointment to Fryerning that the college had enjoyed for some 350 years was brought to an end. The vestry has a memorial to rector Trimble's memory, but the street name, Trimble Close, is the most visible and enduring reminder of his associations with the parish.

It was not only the local Anglican Church that was witnessing changes. In 1917 the new (Catholic) Brentwood Diocese was created, with Ingatestone coming under its jurisdiction. With the return of the Petre family to Ingatestone (see below) regular use of the chapel at Ingatestone Hall must have been made more difficult and in 1922 the Victorian almshouses were repaired and the almshouse chapel was put to greater use.

More significantly, in 1931 the foundation stone was finally laid for a brand new Catholic Church in Ingatestone at the Brentwood end of the High Street. A growing local population and the unavailability of the chapel at Ingatestone Hall meant that the dreams of Canon Last and others would finally be realised. Sebastian Henry Petre, who lived at Tor Bryan (a large house - since demolished - on the site of what is now the Tor Bryan estate) gave both land and £1,000 worth of financial assistance towards the project. The total cost of the building was around £4,000.

The new Catholic church was constructed to the designs of Frank Sherrin, son of George, who deliberately chose red brick as the principal construction material in order to mirror the appearance of the nearby Hall and almshouses. It could house 120 people and some of the furnishings for the new building were transferred from the chapel at Ingatestone Hall, which was itself destined to be removed completely by the 1960s.

In the Petre household in the early 20th century the 13th Lord Petre was succeeded by his brothers, Bernard (1858-1908) and Philip

(1864-1908), as 14th and 15th Lord Petre. The Petre family was still the largest landowner in Ingatestone and the family's ancient ties with the village were reaffirmed when they decided to move back to Ingatestone Hall from Thorndon Hall in 1919 following the death of the 16th Lord Petre, Lionel (1890-1915), during the First World War. Lionel's death occasioned widespread sales from the Petre estates, but most of the family's land in the Ingatestone area was retained because of the move back to the village from Thorndon.

Thorndon Hall had been badly damaged by fire in the late 1870s - apparently necessitating a short stay for the family at Felix Hall, Kelvedon - and another family member, Edward Petre, had died in a plane crash in Yorkshire on Christmas Eve in 1912 when flying from Brooklands to Edinburgh, so it was perhaps felt in any case that a change of scenery was due.

Though Thorndon Hall had been abandoned by the family for day-to-day living, the 9th Lord's biographer, M. D. Petre, could still write in 1928 that the chapel there was "still in use and maintained by the family". She also recorded that it took several days to salvage items from the fire-gutted building, with some papers being saved, plus books from the library and some of the pictures. "The two wings are still standing," she wrote, " - the centre and main portion are an empty shell." After the First World War the east wing was used by Thorndon Park Golf Club, but in recent years the building has been restored and divided up into luxury apartments.

At Ingatestone Lady Rasch, widow of the 16th Lord Petre and mother of Joseph (1914-1989), the 17th Lord Petre, set about trying to return Ingatestone Hall to all its former Tudor glory by removing out-of-character extensions and replacing shoddy workmanship. This was a major undertaking, but the first phase of the work was completed within just three years. More restoration work was carried out in the 1930s and it was during this work that the second priesthole was discovered in what is now the study, the removal of a flue during alterations revealing the long-forgotten hiding place.

Ingatestone was also changing at this time. The old workhouse cottages, which still stand in the High Street just along from the

INGATESTONE, HIGH STREET

High Street, 1905, showing Smith's clock and the buildings in front of the church (r)

Crown public house, were no longer in use for their former purpose. Opposite, the blacksmith's forge or `smithy' was, in 1929, converted into a sweetshop called The Halfway Stop (now The Tuck Shop). Patrick Green's ironmongers (which later diversified into other businesses) was well established between the *Bell* and Makron's (at one time Warder's bakery and now Little Hammonds restaurant) and, further along, opposite the church, G. P. Smith's draper's, furniture and general store was destined to lose its overhanging High Street clock, which was knocked down by a lorry carrying a crane in 1936. The clock had been erected to commemorate one of Queen Victoria's many jubilees, probably her 50th in 1887. The replacement clock, further along the High Street, survived until the 1950s, though its face was altered during the Second World War to delete the word `Ingatestone', in common with the nationwide policy of removing all village names to confuse the enemy in case of invasion. Other notable businesses of the period included F. W. Anger's glass and china shop (a butcher's before Anger's day and now Walker's estate agents) and E. Camp boot and shoe maker (now Hatters).

At the turn of the century the Post Office was in the building next to the alleyway leading from the High Street to the churchyard, now occupied by Pet's Cabin and Vanilla boutique. By 1915 it was employing two telegram boys, but they had only one bicycle between them so they often had to deliver their messages on foot. This could include trips to places as far afield as St Leonard's - an experience, especially in the dark! In 1916 the Post Office was moved to a purpose-built new building (its current location) and the old building was taken over by Mark Wells for his cycle business. The new Post Office building was on land which once belonged to the Writtle Brewery, owners of the nearby *Crown* public house, and right next to the old infants' school (where the library now stands). Just opposite this and a little towards Mountnessing was a private school for both boarders and day pupils: this operated from Ingatestone House from the early 1900s to c.1920.

Just along from this school, where Deep Dene is now, was Samuel Blyth's steam works. Blyth was originally an agricultural engineer and had been born in Springfield in 1856. By 1890 he had moved to Ingatestone and had taken up residence in the house on the corner of Stock Lane opposite the *Anchor*. Corner House was once itself a pub and had also been home to at least two local doctors. Styling himself as an engineer and implement-maker, Blyth had a business in steam cultivation machines, drainage and threshing machines and steam ploughing. The ploughing business really took off and records show that Blyth had ploughing gangs operating all over the county. Two steam ploughing machines were used per field with the plough being suspended on a 600-yard-long cable between them and being passed back and forth as the machines inched along the sides of the field. They could cover five times as much land in a day as could be done with horses or oxen. Blyth also operated a saw bench for cutting up trees for fence posts and other related uses.

There were half a dozen men in a ploughing gang and they would often be away on a job for a fortnight at a time, ploughing the fields from dawn until dusk. They lived in a van attached to the machines where the most junior member of the team, the van boy, cooked their meals and was generally responsible for all the supporting tasks. He would have to get up at 5 o'clock in the morning to stoke up the fire and begin the day's preparations. Van boys generally progressed to driving the machines themselves.

The gang would normally finish the week's work at around lunchtime on a Saturday and its members would walk back to Ingatestone for the weekend, setting out again for the following week's work in the small hours of Monday morning. Samuel Blyth was evidently a bit of a hard taskmaster and would question any gang member whom he encountered in the village when they should have been at work - even if it was 6 o'clock in the morning and there was snow on the ground!

Outside of ploughing season the Ingatestone works were the base for engine overhauls and the de-scaling of boilers, as well as for more domestic repairs such as mending local residents' lawnmowers.

Local services were changing, too. In 1923 the police station was moved a hundred yards or so up the High Street from number 88

Police Station, 1923-1956, High Street

to the big building opposite the church (now Sanders & Company solicitors). This had been purchased for £750 from Charles Alexander Seaton Buist of The Nook, a large house which stood where Bakers Mews is now. Some internal alterations had to be made to convert the building for police use and these were carried out by the firm of G. J. Hawke & Sons. There was later a blue light outside and even today the remains of a low brick wall which used to run along the front of the premises can still be seen.

Amongst the last officers to be stationed at the original police station opposite the *Star* were Sergeant Ball, and PCs Crisp and Fordham. PC Crisp, who joined the force in 1891 and went on to serve 28 years in the Essex Constabulary, earned a merit star for bravery while stationed there. He and a companion, possibly PC Fordham, who may well have been similarly rewarded, were taking a prisoner to Chelmsford when the man broke free, ran towards the railway line and jumped in front of an oncoming train. Both officers leapt after him and pulled him clear as the train rushed by.

The High Street clock on G. P. Smith's shop along from the police station was not the only thing that was knocked down. At the Margaretting end of the village the *Ship* inn, which stood where the Community Club car park is now, was demolished in the early- to mid-1930s. Remembered amongst older residents as a rather salubrious place and the haunt of some dodgy characters, it was also said to have 'the repute of being rather damp, having a well under one of its floors'. The floor was a little lower than the pavement and customers had to step down as they entered. The pub was run for many years by the Dennis and King families, but became Mark Wells's cycle shop when it lost its licence. Wells, who was also the first person in the village to sell petrol (in the old two-gallon cans), later moved his business further down the High Street to the site of the old Post Office (now Pet's Cabin). His son-in-law, Henry King, carried on the cycle business there in later years and is well remembered in the village. The Kings were also wheelwrights, which would seem to tie in rather nicely with the bicycle business.

In the Market Place the *White Hart* (where Chequers is now)

High Street, 1905, with the *White Hart* and The Limes

was also demolished in the mid-1930s, having lost its licence several years earlier. It had briefly been renamed the *Ipswich Arms*, perhaps in an attempt to relaunch it and capture more trade, but it soon reverted to the old name. In its last years the building saw service as a tea-room for a short period, but the end was definitely in sight.

After the inn's demolition the site stood empty for several years, occupied a little later only by a bus shelter and some toilets and with the open space proving increasingly popular as a place for motor cars to park on. Some of the pub's old stables and out-buildings were converted into cottages and a furniture warehouse, used for storage purposes by G. P. Smith and then by Bonds.

Another pub, the *Royal Oak* (where Budgens now stands) lost its licence before the Great War, but its demolition was delayed somewhat longer than its compatriots and it survived long enough to see service as housing until its eventual demolition in the 1970s.

Of other Ingatestone pubs that had already long-since disappeared by this stage, the *Swan* is remembered for its involvement in the late-18th century prizefighting scene, and notably for a contest which took place there in 1789 between George Ingleston (a London brewer) and John Jackson (trainer to the Prince of Wales). Rain had fallen heavily before the fight and made the specially-laid boards in the yard wet and slippery. During the contest Jackson slipped and broke an ankle. Despite Jackson's offer to continue the fight sitting in a chair, the event was not surprisingly abandoned and victory awarded to Ingleston. The *Swan* was opposite the church. There was a pond in the back yard where fish were kept ready for inn customers (a similar arrangement took place at the *Bell*). Another long-lost pub of note was the *Boot* at Beggar Hill, which apparently had connections with the smuggling industry.

Another sign of the olden days in the village which was removed in the first half of the 20th century was the old parish water pump, which stood in the Market Place. This was one of several pumps in the area, with others at Fryerning church, Beggar Hill and the *Viper* in Mill Green. But with increasing improvement in the supply of water around the county the old pumps became redundant and by the end of the Second World War there were methods other than hand pumps which were being harnessed to provide locals with a better and more hygienic water supply.

Springs had long been used as the main source of water locally, many starting in the area at the top end of Fryerning Lane. Water was then piped down into the village to the area opposite the Post Office, behind the houses in Norton Road. Just after the turn of the century a waterworks was built in Fryerning Lane just before the high path on the right over the bypass bridge, a site now occupied by a small estate of large modern houses.

The development of the waterworks proved rather more problematic than had been anticipated. A well was bored through what was thought to be the deepest bit of London Clay known and the engineers expected to reach water at 400 feet down. They drilled a trial borehole to 532 feet without success, but, encouraged by the County Medical Officer for Health, they pressed on to 700 feet, but still without success. On the point of abandoning the well they pressed on to 800 feet, when they eventually struck water. Left to find its natural level, the water settled at 200 feet below the surface, from whence it was pumped out. A waterworks building was constructed, bearing the date 1906 (the completion date). The waterworks closed in the 1950s and the building was used for a time as a home for the Ingatestone fire engine, before that was moved back to the High Street in the early 1970s. The water tower at Mill Green was built in 1937 to supply local water storage facilities for both Ingatestone and Writtle, after boosting at Stock, and to help with pressure regulation problems in the Mill Green area.

The fields behind Ingatestone church, now the Recreation Ground, were still being used for the grazing of sheep in the first half of the 20th century, but the annual fair had fallen into disuse before the First World War and was formally discontinued by an Order of the Council c.1925. The fair on Fryerning Green, which was once so popular that it blocked all the roads in the area, was another that was destined to disappear. The pond just along from this green could at one stage be driven into by horse and cart to give the animals a drink and to tighten up the vehicle's wooden wheels as the water seeped into them.

On the streets, horse and cart traffic was gradually slipping inexorably towards that era which would ultimately see it replaced completely by motorised vehicles for deliveries, public transport and recreation. The fortunes (and futures) of the old village trades of harnessmaker, wheelwright and blacksmith - businesses which had long sustained countless generations of through-traffic - were, like the coaching inns before them, slowly but surely on the wane.

Other industries of interest were the maltings and the brickworks, which stood, respectively, roughly where Maltings Chase and Deepdene are now. Between the two, on the site of the lower part of The Furlongs, were immense sawpits where whole trees would be sawn up, connected at one time with Patrick Green's. Apart from these, the main types of employment locally for Ingatestone people in the first half of the 20th century were as servants and domestics, farm labourers, builders and railway workers. Some men went to the factories in Chelmsford - notably Cromptons, Hoffmans and Marconis - but there was no mass daily exodus to London as now.

New development was also taking place and new roads were being put in. Norton Road, 'the first and only road of artisans' houses', was built c.1901-2 by Tom Green on land owned by Edgar Norton Disney (hence the name). In the 1930s the first section of what became Pemberton Avenue was put in and by this stage the first Council houses in the village had already been erected at least a decade earlier in Fryerning Lane.

The Chase, a big house which stood in the vicinity of what is now Whadden Chase, was built about 1910 as a residential dwelling, but it was to become known many years later as The Chase Hotel, whose banqueting/ballroom and swimming pool facilities were well-patronised by Ingatestone people.

The first scout group in the village was formed in 1908 by Archibald Christy, whose wife helped Wilde with her 1913 history of the locality. The family built and lived at Wellmead in Fryerning Lane. Their daughter, Violet, was to become founder of the Ingatestone & Fryerning Historical and Archæological Society (in 1965) and there were family connections with the well-known Essex naturalist, Miller Christy, who lived at Chignal St James. Miller Christy was involved in excavations of tiles and pottery at Mill Green just before the First World War. The Christy Hall in Pemberton Avenue (built in the 1970s) still bears the family's name.

There were several major commemorations in the first half of the century in Ingatestone. In January 1901 the church bell was tolled to mark with sadness the death of Queen Victoria, the longest-serving monarch in English history. A decade later, the bell was tolled again to mark the death of her son, Edward VII. Muffled peals were rung on the days of both their funerals.

On a lighter note, in 1902 the coronation of Edward VII had been marked by a torchlight procession, a bonfire and a fireworks display and gifts of meat and groceries were handed out to local people. A `parish tea' was held in the grounds of Docklands. Peals were rung on the church bells and pubs like the *Crown* were festooned with flags, bunting and electric lightbulbs spelling out the letters `E. R.'. The *Crown* was run at the time by the Shuttleworth family, who were landlords there for many decades. Apart from the inn business they also operated a profitable sideline in transportation, offering `horses and carriages of every description' and `conveyances [to] meet all trains'.

The railway station at this time would have been very different from today - the current car park was the station yard, a hive of activity, at one time occupied by sidings, and featuring the premises of several well-known local businesses, including Moy's coal company. The cattle pens in the yard remained in regular use up to the First World War, but with changing farming methods their use declined until they were not required at all. Parts of these pens could still be seen after the Second World War. The station was lit by gas lamps and the platforms were shorter than they are now - they have since been extended to accommodate longer commuter trains.

Ingatestone gasworks was down a turning on the right just before the level crossing in Station Lane, where there is now a sign at the entrance to the driveway saying `Private, The Bungalow'. The gasworks cottages are still there. The gasworks was run for many years by members of the Sibree family. There is a nice (possibly apocryphal) story that Mr Sibree, who lived at the gasworks, used to drink in the *Crown* and when his wife wanted him to come home she would turn the diaphragm up and down so that the gas lights in the pub flickered.

The gasworks closed in the late 1920s when the Gas, Light & Coke Company took over, though local streets continued to be lit by gas until after the Second World War, with the supply being piped in from outside the village. There was said to be a good supply of gas in the Hyde area because the landowners there were shareholders of the gas company.

In 1910 the coronation of George V was also cause for local celebration and once again the High Street was criss-crossed with bunting and flags. Union Jacks and St George Crosses hung the length of the street and the festivities matched those which greeted the coronation of the new King's predecessor only eight years earlier.

Coronation parties in those days included a `public tea', which all the village could join in, and numerous games and activities for the children, including sports events and a Punch & Judy Show. The Silver Jubilee of George V in 1935 was another major local event which is well-remembered by old residents, as is the Coronation of George VI in 1937. Events were usually held on what is now the Seymour Field or on Fairfield, where a row of trees was planted to mark the 1937 event. Another popular pastime of the era was dancing. Dances were held at the Drill Hall in Fryerning Lane, (once used by the Territorial Army and now home to Larmar) but the drive across to Ongar for dancing was another widely-remembered option. The hall at the back of the old *Spread Eagle* pub was also used for dances and other functions.

Of course, the most significant events in the lives of most Ingatestone people in the first half of the 20th century were the two World Wars. Many locals fought in these wars and memorials to them can be found inside both parish churches, as they can in parish churches up and down the land. There are also some memorials to specific individuals who lost their lives in these campaigns, notably in the First World War, which occasioned a far greater loss of life than did the Second.

In Ingatestone church there are memorials to members of the Wood family (of whom more later), including Algernon George Newcombe Wood, who was killed at Gallipoli in 1915 at the age of 36 after previously having served in the Boer War. In the recreation ground behind the church there is a Calvary Cross memorial to the dead of the village which, according to the inscription, was erected by 'some of the inhabitants' of Ingatestone and Fryerning. It has been suggested that this surprisingly specific reference may be an allusion to the local Catholic population (the cross stands next to the Catholic burial ground and the site of the old Catholic school).

At Fryerning there are memorials to two members of the Kortright family. The older is to C. J.'s brother Mounteney, a lieutenant in the 3rd (King's Own) Hussars, who died of wounds received in action at Reitfontein Mine, South Africa, in June 1900. The other is to C. J.'s nephew, also Mounteney, the son of the cricketer's older brother, William. He was a lieutenant in the 1st Battalion of the Essex Regiment and served in Gallipoli before being killed in action in France in May 1917. A third member of the family, yet another Mounteney (son of the first Mounteney) was killed at Dunkirk in 1940. The church also contains memorials to Captain Gordon Elton, DSO, of the Irish Fusiliers, who was killed in action at Poelcappelle in November 1917 and Philip Archibald Christy, a lieutenant in the 2nd Battalion of the Essex Regiment, who was killed in Belgium in February 1915 at the age of just 19, having already served in Marne, Aine and Flanders.

Apart from the tragic effects they had on the lives of Ingatestone and Fryerning people, the two World Wars also brought some other changes to the village. With its place on the main highway from London to Colchester, Ingatestone in particular saw much military traffic during the wars. Many soldiers passed through the village - marching all the way from Ingatestone to Harwich - or were billeted

Huskards

there. In a curious echo of earlier history this may have recalled for the very oldest residents the days of the Napoleonic Wars when a similar arrangement had been in operation.

During the Great War soldiers were stationed in what is now the Seymour Field, at the Margaretting end of the village, and many of these, including members of the Nottinghamshire and Worcestershire Regiments, married locally and stayed on in the village.

Troops were also put up locally at several of the big houses in the area. During the First World War soldiers were stationed at Fryerning Hall, whilst Huskards was used as a convalescent home. The Hilder family were the last private residents of Huskards, which is now flats, and between the wars Colonel Hilder was present at the planting ceremony for the tree on Fryerning Green in 1935, which was put in to mark the Silver Jubilee of George V. Colonel Hilder told boys present at the time that they would never live to see it as a fully grown tree, but fortunately some of them did! The Hilders also ran a girls' camp at Huskards for a time.

During World War II soldiers were stationed at the big houses of Ard Tully, Nithsdale and Docklands. The two latter are no longer there, but Ard Tully still stands. Meals for soldiers stationed locally were prepared at a cookhouse in the building in the High Street now home to Shadforth Chemists and Taylor & Company Estate Agents. Mill Green Common and the adjoining woods were used for military training exercises and for the storage of material for D-Day. Some important parades were also held locally, including the Norfolk and Suffolk Regiments' Minden Day parade in 1943 which took place on Fairfield.

Fortunately during the Second World War, when aerial bombardment was more of a threat, Ingatestone and Fryerning both escaped major incident. Some oil bombs were dropped in Norton Road and sprayed oil up the fronts of many of the houses, but the incendiary bombs which were launched behind them with the intention of setting fire to all the dispersed oil, missed their target and a disaster was thankfully averted. Buttsbury church was one of the few buildings locally to be damaged by bombing and was closed

St Mary, Buttsbury

temporarily for services until full repairs could be initiated. The then Ingatestone rector, Geoffrey Foulerton, wrote in the March 1941 issue of the Ingatestone and Fryerning parish magazine that "as regards St Mary's, Buttsbury, I am afraid we must probably consider it closed for the duration of the war. The structural damage is not severe, but the windows are badly shattered; a special effort to restore it would hardly be justified until we had reconsidered the whole problem of this ancient and isolated little church".

Two massive searchlights were installed in the locality to help spot aircraft at night. One of these stood at Beggar Hill, where soldiers were also stationed for a time; the other stood approximately where the roundabout is in Pemberton Avenue, near to the junior school. At the time this area was known as the Searchlight Meadow and was somewhat remote from the road as Pemberton Avenue only extended half a dozen houses up from Fryerning Lane before terminating in a cul-de-sac. At the end of the road and behind the Drill Hall and Boys' School there were fields used for football (where one of the local Ingatestone clubs played) and the Searchlight Meadow was the field beyond that.

In the fields around Wellmead, at the top end of Fryerning Lane, big guns were trained on attacking aircraft and the area was known for a time as Gunfield. Meanwhile, in the Market Place a circular concrete water holder was built, about 40-50 feet in diameter, to provide a local water source in the middle of the village in case any fires were started there as a result of enemy action.

Another area of World War II interest was a military stores depôt which was in the fields between Stock Lane and Margaretting church. Evidence of this remains, in the form of a network of concrete roads, accessible from the lane next to Rays at the Margaretting end of the village, which were originally put in as part of a proposal to build what became known as 'The Asylum' there. This institution, proposed just before the start of the war, was never built and the site was instead taken over for military purposes.

A narrow-gauge railway was laid right across the stores depôt, allowing the transportation of materials all around the site and the last few remaining tracks of the railway are still visible across the concrete in one or two places. The Texaco Star sign was also visible for a time after the war. Some of the original storage tanks are still in use, apparently carrying pesticide for use on the local farm.

Part of this depôt site, between Rook and Spring Woods, was in use before the Second World War as Ingatestone Polo Field. Polo, archery and pony club gymkhana events all took place there in the summer, whilst in winter it was the location for 'dangerous' mixed hockey matches. Vehicular access could formerly be had from Stock Lane (from just opposite where the sewage treatment works are now). The field was ploughed up during the war and the polo pavilion has disappeared. The Essex Archers subsequently held meetings on the playing fields at Felsted School, but the days of polo playing in the village had come to an end. Part of the area was also once used by Flying Fleas - a type of small aircraft popular at the time.

There were, of course, post-war celebrations in the villages after both events were over. In 1919, for example, there was an Armistice Parade through Ingatestone High Street, featuring groups of local children, and buildings like the almshouses were bedecked with bunting. In 1902, after the end of the Boer War, there had also been local celebrations - the flag was raised at Ingatestone church and the bells were rung. Streets were decorated the following day and there was a torchlight procession and bonfire, plus a public meeting in the Market Place featuring rousing speeches by local residents Mr Coverdale, Mr Conybeare and Lieutenant Colonel Wood.

POST WAR DEVELOPMENT

After the Second World War there was something of a building boom in Ingatestone. Parts of the High Street which had been unchanged for centuries took on new identities and many of the old buildings disappeared. The old trades were on their way out, too.

The electrification of the railway, coupled with a period of relative prosperity and peace, brought many new people into the village. The slightly more rural Fryerning escaped much of this post-war development, but central Ingatestone was destined for major change. Writing in the late 1960s Marcus Crouch wrote (somewhat harshly) of the 'overgrown commuter village of Ingatestone' that 'this place must have until recently been charming, but the demands of a suddenly enlarged population have not been met without sacrifice of visual amenities and personality'.

In 1901 the combined population of Ingatestone and Fryerning was just 1,748. By 1991 it had reached 4,815. The increasing population after the War necessitated something of a localised building boom and from the 1950s to the 1970s many new developments sprang up across the village. Many of the large old Victorian houses were swept away and new housing estates were built in their place. Large, old and/or prominent buildings demolished to make way for this new development included Nithsdale (replaced by Ashleigh Court and The Paddocks), The Chase (Whadden Chase and adjoining roads), Tor Bryan (the Tor Bryan estate), The Limes (a new road, shops, a bank and some flats), the *Spread Eagle* (more shops) and Docklands (Docklands Avenue and adjoining roads). Buildings facing the High Street immediately in front of the church were also demolished, to open up a better view of the building, and The Furlongs estate was constructed on the disused brickfields.

The Limes stood opposite the *White Hart* (on the site currently occupied by Martins) and was for many years occupied by local doctors. Earlier in its history it had been a pub called (variously) the *New Inn*, the *Red Lion* and possibly the *Petre's Arms*. It had extensive grounds to the rear but the building itself abutted right onto the main road and had rings in the front wall which were once used for tying horses to. In the 1960s it was declared unsafe and big timbers were put up against the front wall, blocking part of the road. By the 1970s the building had gone and its land had been built on, a new road called The Limes being laid through the site towards the Recreation Ground.

The Roman Catholic school, which stood behind The Limes in Star Lane, was itself replaced by Ingleton's Estate Agents, which in turn became a doctor's surgery (c.1961). This surgery - 'The Folly' - has since been replaced by housing and 'The New Folly' surgery has been erected in Bell Mead.

The Tor Bryan estate was built on the site of Tor Bryan house, named for the place of origin of Sir William Petre, founder of the Essex branch of the family, and once occupied by Sebastian Petre. The houses of somewhat experimental design erected in this exclusive driveway were described at the time of their construction as being both 'before their time' and 'expensive houses of uninhibited design'. Some might say that to the 1990s eye they look rather dated, but they remain classic examples of period architecture.

The old Tor Bryan house had been built as Heybridge House on land belonging to Heybridge Farm, a property in the Petres' ownership which was farmed by the Self family, who also had interests in the maltings and *New Inn*. Sebastian Petre, younger brother of William, 12th Lord Petre, took the lease of Heybridge House from his uncle, the 11th Lord, and renamed it Tor Bryan to distinguish it from Heybridge Farm (now the Heybridge Hotel). After Sebastian's death in 1934 (he was buried at Fryerning) the property was retained by his wife until 1946 when it was sold to Dorothy Howe. It was demolished c.1962 and the land bought by A. Saunders & Company, who spent six years building the distinctive houses to the designs of Design & Manning Associates of Notting Hill Gate.

Docklands was a large house at the Margaretting end of the village on a site now occupied by Docklands Avenue, Park Drive, and Pine Drive and Close. It was built on fields originally called Upper and Lower Dockey (probably named in relation to their size) and was one of the first big houses to be built in the village after the coming of the railway. Its first occupant, in 1859, was a barrister, Frederick Smith, but by 1862 it was in the ownership of Henry Newberry, a retired merchant from Manchester, who was to co-found the Working Men's Club with Reverend Parkin. Newberry died in 1876 and is buried in Fryerning churchyard.

Occupants of Docklands would appear to have been fairly self-sufficient, with fresh milk, eggs, pork, butter, cream, bread and fruit all available on site. The house stood back from the road and had very spacious grounds, accessed by a long driveway bordered by lime trees. The owner's needs were attended to by servants, many of them employed from the local community.

In 1902 the property came into the ownership of Lieutenant Colonel George Wilding Wood, who moved there from another big house, Nithsdale. Wood was a great benefactor to the village, as well as being a JP, a Deputy Lieutenant of Essex and an Ingatestone churchwarden. He hosted village events in the grounds of his house and in 1908 gave a consignment of coal to the poor of the village. The marriage of his daughter Mary was said to have been one of the best-attended events in the village.

Lieutenant Colonel Wood died in 1918. His funeral procession from Docklands to Fryerning church was attended by hundreds of villagers, including Patrick Green and Kate Sherrin, a relative of George. Docklands itself lasted until the 1950s, the only reminders today being the name of Docklands Avenue, a surviving stretch of the boundary wall which once encircled the grounds and a few lime trees which marked out the avenue towards the building.

The Chase Hotel was demolished c.1960. It may have taken its name from associations with the local hunt, or maybe even from an old Roman track which could have existed in the vicinity. The line of the western boundary of Whadden Chase, which was built in its place, is said to have been shaped by the old parish boundary between Ingatestone and Fryerning.

Heybridge Hotel

Nithsdale, another victim of development at this time, may well have once been used as a railway station hotel. The houses in front of the church were demolished in the mid-to-late-1950s and The Furlongs was built in the early 1960s, the new junior school there opening in 1964.

One of the most prominent redevelopments in Ingatestone was surely that right in the centre of the village in the Market Place, once the site of the *White Hart* public house. Cottages to the rear of the old pub site were demolished and a new row of shops, called Chequers, was built on the front of the site, with a public car park and toilets to the rear. A large mosaic was incorporated into the façade of the new building to depict scenes relating to Ingatestone history, including the visit of Queen Elizabeth I to Ingatestone Hall.

Extensive development has also taken place at the south western tip of the village around the area known as Heybridge. The Heybridge Hotel is probably the oldest surviving building in this area, parts of it appearing to date from around 1494. Heybridge Farm and tan yard once occupied part of the site, but by the 1960s it had already become established as a hotel. Many of the buildings in this area, such as those on Heybridge Road, are postwar, but the estate was begun with Rye Walk and The Leas in the late-1920s and 1930s. Nearer the High Street, more recent development has also taken place on the Ingatestone side of Station Lane.

One of the most interesting, if temporary, housing developments in the village was the estate of prefabricated houses at the end of The Meads, commonly known for short as `the prefabs'. These were constructed c.1948 to provide cheap, well-designed postwar housing and were meant to have only a short lifespan, though they actually lasted up to the 1980s (since which time a new estate has been built on the site). The Meads was originally a cul-de-sac and the site on which the prefabs were built was formerly fields used for cattle grazing. The buildings were modern and up-to-date for their time, based on an American idea and incorporating the forerunners of the modern fitted kitchen. There was once a whole series of ponds in the area, stretching from the Meads to Pemberton Avenue, and cattle grazing on the fields would often get trapped in the marshy ground and have to be pulled out by tractors. The Meads was chosen as the site for the prefabs because the road had already been constructed - The Meads development had been started c.1937 to provide low-cost local housing, but had come to a halt at the start of the War.

Perhaps the most lamented loss during this period of intensive redevelopment was the old *Spread Eagle* coaching inn - a magnificent building which would probably have been saved today as a result of increasing environmental awareness and a growing conservation movement. The *Spread Eagle* - formerly just the *Eagle* - was one of the few surviving symbols of the coaching era. A classic coaching inn in the old style - and of significant architectural merit - it attracted plaudits for its design from no lesser authority than the *Buildings of England* author, Nikolaus Pevsner, who liked, in particular, the sign showing it to be a `Commercial Inn and Posting House', which he praised for its especially noteworthy early Victorian lettering.

The inn's land, which stretched back towards the railway line and was used for the stabling and grazing of horses, has also been built on (Ingleton House is there now) and the `enormous pond' which once existed there has also disappeared. There were once also extensive outbuildings in the cobbled inn yard, in the upper stories of which travellers sometimes slept if there was no room in the main building. The site is now occupied by the Co-op, a hairdressers and a launderette and only the name - in Spread Eagle Place - and a few old photographs survive to remind us that there was once an inn there at all.

Across the road, the old *Royal Oak*, which had later been used as private residences, was also demolished. The site stood empty for a short time and became the location for a Barclays Bank temporary portacabin, whilst the bank's main building was undergoing refurbishment. The site is now occupied by Budgens supermarket.

The *Spread Eagle* was the most recent of the old Ingatestone pubs to be demolished. There were once 27 pubs in Ingatestone and Fryerning, the list reading: *Anchor, Bell, Bird-in-Hand* (later *Queen's*

120

Corner House and the old Post Office

Head), Blue Boar, Boot, Bull, Chequers, Cock, Cricketers' Arms, Crosskeys, Crown, Davy, Dolphin, Duke's Head, Eagle, George, Lion, Maypole, New Inn, Royal Oak, Ship, Star, Swan, Viper, White Hart, White Horse and *Woolpack.* Now only seven remain: the *Anchor, Bell, Crown* and *Star* in Ingatestone High Street and the *Cricketers, Viper* and *Woolpack* in Fryerning and Mill Green.

Even the surviving *Anchor* is not the original pub, but a new building on a site set slightly back from the original, which had to be demolished when Stock Lane was widened. This may have been necessary because of the erection of the original railway station in Stock Lane, or it may have been slightly later.

The *Crown* was for many years known as the `inn at the end of the town' - the last building at the south western end of the High Street before the fields. As time went on the Shuttleworth family's horse and carriage business there evolved into a modern taxi service. Prospective customers would wait in a little room at the side of the inn whilst the taxi was being prepared.

There is a romantic story that a runaway princess stayed in one of the Ingatestone pubs when trying to escape her pursuers, but since different sources quote it as being both the *Bell* and the *Spread Eagle* the lack of certainty unfortunately casts a bit of doubt on the subject.

The loss of many of these historic buildings in Ingatestone may well be lamented, but the other side of the coin was that the village gained a number of new facilities. The supermarkets which replaced the inns were welcome additions to the lively shopping centre, whilst at the Mountnessing end of the High Street a new library was built next to the Post Office on the site of the old infants' school.

New schools also appeared. A new infants' school was built at the end of Fryerning Lane on land behind the old Girls' School and a new junior school was built in The Furlongs in 1964 to replace both the old Girls' School and the old Boys' School, which were in Fryerning Lane between the entrance to Steen Close and what is now the Larmar building. The infants shared temporarily with the juniors until the new infants' school opened in 1969.

The Anglo-European School

There was also a brand new secondary modern school in Willow Green, one of the many new roads that was formed around the village during the century. Built in 1959 for 370 pupils it was enlarged and reopened in 1973 as the Anglo-European School, with a heavy emphasis on Europe-related activities and a greatly increased capacity of around 1,000 pupils. Preference in terms of selection for attendance at the school is given to pupils who have a demonstrable interest in, or proven connections with, other parts of Europe. There are 20 similar schools across the country and the Anglo-European has an extensive exchange programme with schools in continental countries - so extensive that the normal curriculum is often suspended and replaced with an alternative programme when exchange visits are under way. Students and teachers both take part in these exchanges.

Anglo-European students are from the parishes of Ingatestone & Fryerning, Margaretting and Mountnessing and partly from outlying parts of Essex. Many are also non-UK nationals. Language training is a fundamental part of the education programme and the school recently piloted a worldwide French examination. Since 1978 the International Baccalaureate has also been offered as an alternative to A-levels. Work experience in European countries is available. The school's stated aim is to provide 'the highest quality national education enriched by a European and international ethos'.

With a growing population, the infrastructure supporting the village had also to be improved. The fire engine was moved from the site of the old waterworks in Fryerning Lane to a new station in the High Street. It had already been housed in the vicinity once before, having even earlier been housed in the Market Place and the south porch of the church. With the advance of technology, the method of call-out progressed from maroons, to bells in firemen's houses to modern pagers.

A new purpose-built police station was also constructed at the Margaretting end of the village in the late 1950s/early 1960s to a standard design for police stations which had been adopted through-out the county. The station strength of a sergeant and two constables remained, the sergeant living in the house attached to the station; the constables in the pair of semi-detached houses alongside.

Whilst a considerable amount of development has taken place in Ingatestone throughout the 20th century, Fryerning has been largely spared the developers' attentions. One of the few imposing buildings to be lost there this century was the Disneys' 18th century mansion, The Hyde, which was used for a short time as a school before it was destroyed by fire in 1965.

Many of the newer roads have been named in honour of well-known local people, a positive and very commendable policy adopted by the parish council. Disney Close was named after the Disney family, whilst Pemberton Avenue, Trimble Close and Mellor Close all take their names from local clergymen. Wadham Close was named for the Wadham family, whilst Exley Close is named after a local councillor and Steen Close after a local doctor.

In addition to the many new roads laid out within the village, there was the much larger bypass project which was constructed around the north western side of central Ingatestone. Even before the Second World War there had been those who had suggested that a bypass should be built. The Ministry of Transport had even purchased what became known as the Transport Meadow (now the Seymour Field) with this very aim in mind.

The 1930s had seen cars becoming increasingly popular, particularly with the advent of vehicles like the £100 Ford which brought motoring within reach of ordinary people. The road through Ingatestone village was very busy with coastal traffic, particularly at the weekends with day trippers taking outings to the east coast resorts of Clacton and Walton. Coaches thundered through the village in large numbers (motorised now, not horse-drawn) and there was even a policeman on point duty at the Fryerning Lane/Stock Lane junction to prevent the situation degenerating into chaos. On a Sunday evening, with all the traffic returning from the resorts, it was even difficult to cross the road.

The construction of the bypass was a major undertaking, costing several hundred thousand pounds, a large sum in those days. A whole swathe of land between Ingatestone and Fryerning was cut open and a handful of cottages standing north of Trimble Close had to be demolished.

The official bypass opening ceremony was held in November 1959. The Minister of Transport cut the tape across what was described as 'the two-mile-long dual carriageway bypass on the A12 London-Great Yarmouth trunk road' and the chairman of Essex County Council told those in attendance that it was the first stretch of dual road in open country on the east coast route out of London. Generous provision of laybys had been made 'to prevent parking on the bypass', Reverend Hudson (Ingatestone rector from 1952 to 1989) conducted a short service and even wrote a special hymn dedicated to road safety and courtesy. For a time Ingatestone was relatively traffic free, but even today it still has its busy periods.

A useful by-product of bypass construction was that the new road gave Ingatestone an immovable north-western boundary which, coupled with the railway on the south-eastern side of the village, effectively served to limit the boundary of available development land to within the village centre. All substantial development which has taken place in the village since this time has been limited to land between these two markers, thankfully protecting the countryside beyond from any further encroachment by Mankind.

The advance of the motor car had been rapid. Before the First World War the Shuttleworth family at the *Crown* was still taking its passengers to the railway station by horse and cart. Even into the 1950s the pace of life was slow and the horse and cart was still a regular sight. Today the motor car holds sway.

"Life in the village is far duller than of old," wrote Mrs Wilde in 1913, "in spite of daily papers and the penny post; and the thousands of excursionists who whisk through our parish glean little pleasure from us, and we none at all from them. Silence has fallen upon the highway, save for the roar of a passing train or the rattle of a motor, and you may drive to Chelmsford and meet no more than a dozen carts and a handful of wayfarers."

One cannot help wondering what she would make of it all now.

126

POSTWAR VILLAGE LIFE

The period of redevelopment that was going on ln the village after the Second World War was the biggest time of change for Ingatestone since the early 18th century, when new buildings were being erected in numbers to accommodate the increasing coaching trade. The physical shape of the place may have been changing around them after the war, but life for the inhabitants still went on.

In 1952 Edward Hudson was appointed as Reverend Foulerton's successor. He was to serve the village for 37 years until his death in January 1989 at the age of 82. Hudson was born in Bradford in June 1906, but was educated in Norfolk when his family moved to Great Yarmouth. He grew to love that adopted county and still visited it regularly even when installed in Ingatestone. He studied at Durham University and was a keen cricketer and reader.

In 1937 Hudson was appointed curate of St Margaret's, Barking, where he stayed until in 1947 he became Director of Education in the Church (a post he was to hold until 1955) and in 1949 he was appointed vicar of Dengie & Asheldham. He held this post until moving to Ingatestone in 1952. Reverend Hudson began to make his presence felt in Ingatestone from the start. The year after his appointment he instituted a new annual custom of having the choir sing from the church tower first thing in the morning - a custom which was to gain national media attention in later years.

In 1956 he oversaw some more repairs to Ingatestone church tower, using 5,000 bricks given by Essex County Council from the recently-demolished Belhus mansion in Aveley. Two years later the ecclesiastical anomalies between the Ingatestone and Fryerning parish boundaries were finally ironed out, whilst in the 1960s the rectory was redecorated and restored and central heating was introduced.

Reverend Hudson and his wife operated an open house policy during his incumbency and the rectory and its grounds were often used for parties, fêtes, picnics, prizegiving ceremonies and other parish events. (This was the Fryerning Lane rectory. The old rectory in Fairfield, which had been a private house since the turn of the century when rector Earle was the incumbent, was demolished in 1968 to make way for the Fairfield housing estate.)

1968 also saw the arrival of some new pews at Ingatestone from the redundant church of Dr Barnado's Garden City at Woodford Green. The previous year had seen the insertion of steel plates in the wall between the south chapel and chancel. New floor tiles and some remodelling of the glass entrance doorway under the tower also took place around this time.

In 1970 Thomas Scarfe's 1780 hand-wound clock mechanism was replaced by an electric one, Scarfe's being removed to Chelmsford museum. Yet more improvements were made in 1974, with the construction of new vestries and toilet facilities beyond the north (Petre) chapel, which had of necessity itself been in use as a somewhat cluttered vestry for several years previously.

In 1972 floodlights were provided to illuminate the tower at night. Six years later the church flag was flown at half-mast on the death of the Pope and in 1982 the church celebrated its 900th anniversary. This was an approximate but probably fairly accurate date, chosen in part because some additional restoration work was completed in that year and possibly also in part because it marked the 30th anniversary of Reverend Hudson's incumbency.

Hudson died in 1989 and was replaced by the current incumbent, Philip Coulton. A detailed coloured plan of the church, showing dates of construction of various parts of the fabric, hangs inside the building to Reverend Hudson's memory. A more permanent memorial to him has also been discussed, but has not been instituted at the time of writing.

At Fryerning, Reverend Trimble was succeeded in 1957 by William (`Billy') Mellor. Mellor was the first incumbent to be appointed in joint control of both Fryerning and Margaretting parishes, as rector of the former and vicar of the latter. Before Fryerning, he had been rector of Chignal Smealey, vicar of Roxwell and Hospital Chaplain at St John's in Chelmsford (he was to continue in the latter role for a total service time of 45 years).

Before that he had worked in South Africa. He died in 1979 and is buried in Fryerning churchyard.

Reverend Mellor is remembered locally both as a jovial man and for his 'homely sermons'. His obituary in the Ingatestone & Fryerning parish magazine, *The Tower* (August 1979), recalled him as having "a huge warm heart... an uncommonly even temper, a quick wit... [and] a huge voice if the singing faltered"! At times he would even share his home with those less privileged than himself. The Bishop of Bradwell wrote in the same magazine that "it will be hard to imagine life here without him". His wife Gwen, a doctor, whom he had met at St John's, later worked in the Blood Transfusion Service in Brentwood. She died in 1996. The street name, Mellor Close, is a reminder of the couples' contribution to the community.

Reverend Mellor was succeeded in 1980 by John Gravelle, the role of the incumbent now being referred to as 'priest-in-charge' rather than 'rector'. Gravelle, whose father was Welsh, was a chorister in the Chapel Royal and studied at Durham University, where he passed two BAs in Philosophy and Theology. He spent some time in the army during the war and later served in Cyprus.

In later life he trained as a psychotherapist at the Tavistock Clinic in Hampstead, which was run by Dr Frank Lake, who pioneered the study of the relationship between psychology and religion. Reverend Gravelle became his disciple and Deputy Director of the Clinic and dealt with cases of clergymen who were suffering from domestic or psychological problems. He was an assistant at the Chelmsford Cathedral Centre, specialising in psychological problems. He often made trips to the south coast to talk to nuns about religious matters. Always a busy man, he also somehow managed to fit getting married (to Kathleen, a Chelmsford teacher) and bringing up four children around his very full career.

Reverend Gravelle retired to Chelmsford when his stint at Fryerning came to an end in 1989 and he is remembered by his parishioners for his gift of understanding people and their problems and for his 'marvellous deep voice and eloquence'.

In 1989, with the death of Reverend Hudson at Ingatestone and the retirement of Reverend Gravelle at Fryerning, an attempt was made after a few months of discussion to set up a Team Ministry covering the five parishes of Ingatestone & Buttsbury, Fryerning & Margaretting and Mountnessing. Reverend Philip Coulton was appointed head of the Team Ministry, with primary responsibility for Ingatestone and Buttsbury, and Reverend Christopher Martin was appointed under him as Team Vicar of Fryerning, Margaretting and Mountnessing. Although these arrangements were made, however, they were only really provisional and the merger never fully took place. It was never popular with churchgoers, Mountnessing was never properly taken into the arrangement and the short spell that Reverend Martin spent in the locality (three years until 1992) meant that the situation required some further consideration.

Reverend Martin is remembered as a clever man who was educated through Marlborough College public school and Trinity College, Oxford. He came into the Church rather late in life after a career as a journalist. He was editor of various religious magazines and appeared on television and radio as a religious adviser. He visited Jerusalem and wrote several books. He left Fryerning (and Margaretting) to go to St Ippolyts church at Ippollitts, Hertfordshire.

One other notable change in local Anglican Church affairs during this period was the demolition of the `new' rectory in Fryerning Lane shortly after Reverend Hudson's death and the building of Rectory Close containing five large detached houses in its place. The current rectory is one of these houses.

Since 1992, when Reverend Martin left Fryerning, Reverend Coulton has continued as priest-in-charge of Ingatestone and Buttsbury, whilst Reverend Canon John Brown has come from Kelvedon Hatch to take over as priest-in-charge of Fryerning, Margaretting and Mountnessing, as well as operating as the Diocesan Rural Officer. There is still a possibility that the idea for linking the five parishes into a Team Ministry may once again raise its head, but at the time of writing there is no confirmation of this. Steps have recently been taken to give Buttsbury more independence from Ingatestone, including the establishment of its own church council, but ecclesiastically the two are still firmly united.

The Catholic Church has also seen some changes in the village since the Second World War. By the 1970s the almshouses on the high road had fallen into some disrepair and were, in any case, 'far below acceptable modern standards'. The almshouse charity did not, however, have any capital funding available to enable it to carry out the necessary improvements and, with the additional problem that it had become increasingly difficult to find tenants, the future of the charity looked bleak. Fortunately, however, several organisations combined to provide grants and loans. The Brentwood Diocese, for example, gave a significant sum in return for the right to use available apartments for retired priests. Following the success of this financial input, the almshouses continue to operate as a charity with a Board of Trustees (of which the current Lord Petre is chairman) so none of the dwellings now remain empty for long.

In 1982 the Catholic Church in Ingatestone also held a massive celebration. The year marked the 250th anniversary of the establishment of a Catholic Mission in the village, the 150th anniversary of Canon Last's appointment at Ingatestone Hall and the 50th anniversary of the opening of the new, long-awaited Catholic Church.

The Congregational Church in Ingatestone was also celebrating its long associations with the village in the second half of the 20th century. The original chapel in the High Street had been erected in 1812 and enlarged in 1816, though there had been calls for the establishment of such a church in Ingatestone since at least as early as 1803. Benjamin Hayter was an early campaigner and he and his peers were evidently successful since the increase in attendance soon required that a new chapel should be built. This had been done in 1840, partly on land given by Benjamin Hogg and partly on land covering the old graveyard. The church hall (used for a time as a Sunday School) had been added in 1876 and the manse (a house for the minister) in 1897.

The church celebrated its 150th anniversary in 1962 and evolved into the United Reform Church in the early 1970s following the national merger of the Congregationalists and the Presbyterians. The building still appears in reprints of old pictures as the 'Independent Chapel, Ingatestone Street, Fryerning', a slightly misleading description these days but accurate at the time of the pictures, when much of Ingatestone High Street was still in Fryerning parish.

Ingatestone Hall also underwent several changes after the Second World War. It saw service briefly as a school and then, in the 1950s, the north wing was let to Essex County Council for the storage of historical archive material and the hosting of various summer educational exhibitions, the first of which took place in 1954. In 1961 an Elizabethan Exhibition at the Hall was visited by Queen Elizabeth, the Queen Mother, to mark the 400th anniversary of Queen Elizabeth I having stayed there as a guest of Sir William Petre in 1561. The lease arrangement with the County Council came to an end at the end of the 1970s.

Since 1989, the 17th Lord's son, John (1942-date), has been head of the family as 18th Lord Petre. In recent years the Hall has, amongst other things, played host to an episode of the TV series, *Lovejoy*, and has been open to the public on a regular basis during the summer months since 1993. Many of the original 16th century rooms in the house and the extensive gardens are open for viewing.

In the village, the old trades of blacksmith, wheelwright and saddlemaker all died out completely after the Second World War (although Ingatestone Forge next to Rose's sweetshop still operates a decorative ironwork business). But this was really the inevitable conclusion of a decline that had set in several decades earlier.

George Huffey's wheelwright business in the Market Place was one which was destined to disappear. Huffey worked alone, up to his ankles in shavings, transforming whole trees into completed carts. Local boys used to stand at the door and watch him wielding his spokeshave.

George Downes' blacksmith business was another to disappear. Downes had operated from the old blacksmiths in the High Street

The old blacksmith's

before transferring his business to premises in Fryerning Lane - once the site of Haslers Mill and now Haslers Court. Downes would lift up the horses' hooves, mark out the nail positions and then make custom-fitting steel horseshoes all on the premises.

Haslers themselves were corn and seed merchants waggons used to roll in and out of their premises and they had a garage in Bakers Lane (now HCR Electrical Services). They later progressed to Pierce Arrows lorries. Haslers had two mills in Fryerning Lane, one on either side of the road. Haslers Court is built on the site of the newer mill, which closed in the early 1970s after approximately 30 years of use. Millers Mews is built on the site of the older mill, which survived from the First World War until the early 1980s. Haslers stopped trading in the village in the mid-1970s.

Horse and cart traffic was, of course, in general disappearing. The last of the horse-drawn coalcarts was operated by Mr Wilson of Disney Close. His horse knew its way home from the High Street and on one occasion decided to make the journey without waiting for its owner - and pulled the shaft of the cart through the window of Manning's ironmongers/hardware store, which stood where Ingatestone Dry Cleaners is now. The last person in the village to use horse transport on a regular basis is said to have been Henry Atkinson, who operated a pony and trap.

Other local businesses and businessmen are remembered fondly by older residents. Reg Vince, for example, had a wooden grocer's shop in the Market Place, where Ingatestone Pet Shop is now. He sold, amongst other things, broken biscuits and sugar weighed in a blue bag and later had a brick building erected. Next door there was Wallbanks newsagents (now the dentist). Across the road where the car park is now was Jimmy Westle's garage. Jimmy was also one of the two local taxi drivers (Jack Shuttleworth of the *Crown* was the other). He lived for many years with his mother in one of the houses that used to stand in front of the church. Cheeses for Reg Vince's shop were stored in premises behind Jimmy Westle's garage and the Saturday boy would roll them, wrapped in hessian, across the road from storeroom to shop.

Elsewhere in the village there was Green's Stores (now Wine Rack), Luckin Smith's (later a Budgens and now the Nirvana Indian Restaurant) and Percy Greenfield's (currently unoccupied, next to Taylor & Company Estate Agents). Other well-known businesses included Manson's butchers (formerly Hugh Wright's and now Gordon Electronic Repairs), the old Co-op butchers (next to Barclays) and Stamford's (next to where Percy Greenfield's was). What is now the Carlok Garden fish and chip shop has been variously Flo's Café, the Tivoli Café and the Norfolk Tearooms. Next door (now the upholsterers) was George Camp's shoe repair shop. Camp would sit there with a mouthful of nails, hammering away at his shoes. Along the same stretch of the High Street were the dairy (where the bookshop is now) and Mrs Ball's sweetshop, which was a popular stopping-off place for children after the traditional Sunday afternoon family walk.

Mark Wells' cycle shop (now Pet's Cabin) was being run by his son-in-law, Henry King, and Moy's Coal company also had an office on the premises at one stage. The building next door, adjacent to the churchyard, used to be a doctor's and still bears the name, 'The Old Surgery'. What is now Dibble's furniture restorers was once a general store, with a hairdressers at the back which was separated from the main shop by a curtain.

Walker's Estate Agents in the Market Place was formerly an antiques shop and then a china and glass shop run by F. Anger; it had also once been a butcher's. On the opposite corner E. Camp's boot and shoe repairers (now Hatters) became a cafe and just along from that there was Pledge's sweetshop and hairdressers, now Chelsea China. Bairstow Eves was formerly a toy shop and there was a baker's at the Market Place end of Bakers Lane (hence the name).

Where Bell Mead is now there was a jewellery factory run by the Pritchard brothers - a strange-looking building remembered as being enclosed and dark and secret. Nearby, in what is now Avrohurst Village Services (the video shop) was Thurgoods TV and electrical store. Opposite that was Thurgoods grocers, which was also a wet fish business for a time. The Thurgoods - Jack and Fred - were brothers. Security Insurance was the Beehive Woolshop and the Gemini fine art shop was a shoeshop.

Across the road, next to the *Crown* was Mr Scales' shoe repairers (now K. J. Electrical). Opposite that, the Congregational Chapel Manse on the corner of Norton Road was rented out to various local doctors and just up from there next to Ingatestone House was the Yorkshire Tea Rooms. On the other side of the road, in one of the big houses just along from the library, was Sinclair's dentists.

Along from the Yorkshire Tea Rooms was a wet fish shop (now Cameron Antiques), which was run at different times by Mr Sexton and Mr Hayes. Lorries used to bring in great big blocks of ice, which were swung around by large metal hooks and broken down into pieces to be put with the fish to keep it fresh. Before the Second World War the building had been an electrical shop and earlier still a carpenter's.

Where Deep Dene is now was a commercial market garden and smallholding, run by Ted Green. Adjacent to this was Tom Green's sawyer business, on the site which had been Sammy Blyth's steam works. There were often fires in the pits where sawdust from sawing was tipped because the sawdust generated its own heat. Children would also burrow down into it and find that it got hotter and hotter the deeper they went. There was also at one time a sectional shed business on the site.

It was in this area, too, that during and after the war the local fire station was located (the current station is just a short distance away). The fire engine was kept in a barn and manned by auxiliary firemen. The office was permanently staffed by two ladies who manned the telephones. The engine was often used as back-up for main stations if their engines were out on a shout. This was in the days before a standard driving test was required and the test for driving the fire engine involved going out with the leading firemen and 'if you got it back safely, you passed the test'! All the firemen had bells in their houses (apparently to differentiate a fire alarm from the sound of wartime sirens). The fire engine was later moved to the old waterworks building in Fryerning Lane.

The area from Deep Dene on towards the Furlongs and beyond was also home to the village brickfields and maltings, as well as to Moy's coalyard. The brickfields probably stopped operating around the time of the First World War, but remnants of them were still visible in the 1940s. The engine sheds and engines were still there and children used to slide down the old belt shutes. The kilns were still there then, too, as were the big rectangular pits from which brick earth was cut. On part of the site was a general public refuse tip, known as Ray's Dump after the greengrocer, Mr Ray, who operated from a mobile shop near to where the entrance to The Furlongs is now.

Another feature of postwar village life was the 'Dinner Centre' between The Meads and Norton Road, to which children from all three schools (Boys', Girls' and Infants') used to walk for their daily lunchtime meal. Opposite this was a patch of open ground that was used for Bonfire Night celebrations, while another popular local entertainment was the weekly film show at the Community Club.

Although the High Street has changed a great deal over the years there are still one or two long-established businesses that have survived into the 1990s. These include Fincham's butchers and Raven's bakery. Both Fincham's and Manson's at one time had their own slaughterhouses behind their respective shops.

Outside the village centre there was Kate Camp's shop and a Post Office next to the *Cricketers* inn at Mill Green. At one time there were 16 places to buy cigarettes in the village. Mr Tidyman ran a milk delivery service, via horse and cart, and had a big churn with a brass knob on top from which he filled people's jugs.

Another local character was Gypsy Cable, who carried a watch round with him even though he could not tell the time. Boys would cheekily ask him what the time was and he would show them his watch and reply, "You tell me and then I won't be lying to you".

One of the biggest but perhaps not immediately obvious changes of the century in the locality has taken place in the agriculture industry, in which the local situation has mirrored what has happened on a national basis. Despite the increase in population and the corresponding increase in residential development there is still a healthy concentration of agricultural land in both Ingatestone and Fryerning, though the methods used in the industry are vastly different now from what they used to be. In farming generally, machinery has replaced man as the principal tool of the farmer on both cost and productivity grounds and the number of individuals employed locally on the land has greatly declined, even since as recently as the 1950s. Fields have become larger and there has also been a move towards specialisation to the extent that the day of the traditional mixed farm is now considered to be over.

At Ingatestone Hall, for example, the Petre Estate used to have a dairy herd and a pig unit as well as growing sugar beet and potatoes. Now it does none of those, but concentrates on the production of cereals and other crops harvested by combine, as do most farms in the area. The use of chemical fertilisers and pesticides has accelerated the trend away from diversity as the traditional method of balancing the demands on the land by practising crop rotation is no longer necessary. Using livestock to fertilise the land is no longer a pre-requisite for successful crop growing.

There has, of course, always been some crop growing in the area. During the harvest following the hot dry summer of 1911 fields full of corn of all hues `from the palest yellow to the deepest red gold' could be seen in every direction from the high land at Fryerning. Wheat and oats were the main crops then, as were beans and potatoes. At this time, too, dairy farming was widely practised in the locality, with a flourishing railway trade in milk bound for the Capital being an important aspect of the local economy. The sight of milk-laden carts rushing to meet the train at Ingatestone station was a common one in the village. Cows, too, were often taken by rail to London, initially being bound up in sacks on the station platform and later being given a bit more dignity by being placed in specially provided cattle pens which stood on the right by the down platform where the car park is now.

One of the most visible reminders of the old-style farming industry is the windmill at Mill Green. Built in 1759 on the site of an earlier mill it worked until at least 1905, milling flour for both customers in the village and more distant trade via the highway. In the old days the mill's tailpole had a chain on it, which could be pulled by a donkey to turn it into the wind. It stood for many years in a derelict state, but was rebuilt in 1959, exactly 200 years after its construction, by the owner, Richard Collinson. Much of the work was carried out by C. J. Smith Ltd of Abridge, whilst the oak timber was supplied by W. & C. French of Loughton. The timber was usually shaped at Abridge, but cut to precise dimensions in the vicinity of the mill.

There had been many `running repairs' to the mill over the previous decades, including some carried out by the millwright, Fell Christy. In 1878 a barrel of tar (for repairs) was purchased from Ingatestone Gas Company. Despite some more recent damage during a storm in 1976, the mill survives as a reminder of the past and is now a listed building.

While on the subject of agriculture and land it should be noted that Fairfield has evolved into the Recreation Ground (`the Rec') and its rôle as pasture land for sheep - still active during World War II - has gradually given way to the cricket pitch, the children's playground and a general open space recreation amenity.

Ingatestone and Fryerning have been home to several well-known people during the latter half of the 20th century. Vera Pemberton is covered in her own separate chapter later, whilst two who have achieved fame on a national scale are the MP, Airey Neave, who was murdered by terrorists in 1979 in the precincts of the House of Commons, and the actress, Sarah Miles.

Airey Neave was born in London on 23rd January 1916, the son of Sheffield Airey Neave, a well-known entomologist and honorary secretary of the Zoological Society. The family lived at Mill Green Park in Fryerning.

Airey Neave was educated at Eton and Merton College, Oxford. He subsequently joined the Territorial Army Royal Artillery in 1939 and took part in the battle for Calais during the British retreats in France in May 1940, an experience which he later described in his book, *The Flames of Calais* (1972). He was wounded during the fighting and taken prisoner. He escaped from the prison camp at Torun, but was recaptured in Poland, where he had great admiration for the Poles. He was interrogated by the Gestapo, an experience which made him a great advocate of freedom under the laws of any country and which later ensured that he was to take an active interest in the political situation in Northern Ireland. After interrogation he was sent to the maximum security prison at Colditz, from which he eventually managed to escape in 1942. An account of his experiences in Colditz is given in his book *They Have Their Exits* (1953).

Back in England, Neave made use of the invaluable intelligence information that he had brought back with him by joining MI9 to help underground movements and give guidance to aircrews on how to escape. His time here is recorded in *Saturday at MI9* (1969). By the end of the war Neave had been given many honours, including the MC and the DSO. In 1947 he was given an OBE.

When the War was over he became assistant secretary to the International Military Tribunal and thus, as a lieutenant-colonel, served the charges on the main Nazi war criminals. His last book, *Nuremberg* (1978), covers this period. From 1949 to 1951 he was in command of Intelligence School No.9 (TA), which later became 23 SAS Regiment.

As time went on, his thoughts began to turn to politics. After two unsuccessful attempts - at Thurrock in 1950 and Ealing North in 1951 - he was finally elected Conservative MP for Abingdon in July 1953. He occupied posts as parliamentary private secretary to, initially, the Colonial Secretary and then to the Minister of Transport, which he followed with parliamentary under-secretary at the Air Ministry in 1959.

His interest in science led to him becoming a governor of Imperial College (1963-1971) and a member (and sometime chairman) of the House of Commons select committee on science and technology (1965-75). He was also chairman of the British Standing Conference on Refugees (1972-4) and a UK delegate to the

United Nations High Commissioner for Refugees (1970-5).

Under Margaret Thatcher, with the Conservatives as Opposition Party, he was made head of her private office and shadow secretary of state for Northern Ireland. His murder by Irish terrorists on the ramp of the House of Commons car park by a bomb hidden in his car shocked the world, as it did the people of Fryerning where he had lived for some time as a boy.

A memorial window in Fryerning church records Airey Neave's connection with the village. The window was dedicated in 1985 by the then Bishop of Chelmsford, John Trillo.

The actress Sarah Miles was born at Mill House in Fryerning, though the family later moved to another local property, Barn Mead (formerly called The Tiles and once occupied by the Kortrights). Her family was fairly wealthy and knew both the Petre family and members of the Royal Family, since the Queen Mother was the actress's mother's great-aunt. Her autobiography gives details of her life and times in the village and an insight into the close-knit community. For example, the family had a Rolls-Royce and were once travelling along Ingatestone High Street when they nearly had an accident. "There were only a couple of onlookers," she recalls, "to witness this charade, but in a small community, one is sufficient."

During other escapades, in an old Austin 7, she would take to the country lanes around the village at a very young age without fear of being spotted by the police because the area was considered to be just too rural for the officers to bother with! Both Sarah's brothers went into TV and theatre as well, whilst the actress, Anneka Willis, who appeared in the TV programme, *The Railway Children*, often visited Barn Mead. Sarah's films include *Those Magnificent Men In Their Flying Machines, Ryan's Daughter* and *White Mischief*.

Sarah Miles no longer lives in the village, but another celebrity living in the area and can often be seen jogging or cycling around the country lanes locally is the Essex and England cricketer, Graham Gooch - a prolific batsman with numerous scoring records to his name, who has captained both the county and national sides. He has received an OBE in recognition of his services to cricket.

Several lesser known Essex cricketers also had Ingatestone connections, including Leonard Womersley and Ronald Harvey, who were both born in the village. Another well-known figure in the village was James Wentworth Day, author of several books about Essex and its wildfowling.

The latter half of the 20th century has also seen several major events in the village. In 1946 there was a special Gala Day, organised by the British Legion, when the Dagenham Girl Pipers were the star attraction. The Legion was also responsible for reinstating the Ingatestone Flower Show, which had suffered a temporary decline during the war and which developed into one of the biggest annual events in the village. In its heyday the Flower Show included a `glorious funfair' and there were children's competitions for picking and displaying wild flowers and a whole range of sports events and activities. It is only in the last decade or so that the event has been toned down, apparently because it was beginning to attract groups of noisy youths from outside the village, a fact which local residents who lived near the Seymour Field (where it was held) did not appreciate. A handful of flower shows and other events had also been held in a meadow off Station Lane (which had doubled as the home pitch for Ingatestone Rovers Football Club) and at The Hyde (which is also remembered for hosting fairs and horse shows). In the early years of football on the Seymour Field (then called the Transport Meadow) the players had to share their pitch with cows from a local farm - making a clear-up job before the game got under way an essential part of pre-match preparations!

Another major post-war event was the coronation of Queen Elizabeth II, which was celebrated in traditional style in 1953. The celebrations included a `Pageant of Two Parishes', written by V. M. Christy, and a ring of trees, brought specially from Danbury, was planted on the right of the path leading from the Recreation Ground to Ingatestone station. The fact that it poured with rain all day did not dampen the spirits too much.

It rained even harder in September 1958, when Essex was hit with a torrential downpour. The brook under the High Street near the *Bell* burst its banks and flooded out into Pudneys' woodyard, which stood opposite. Planks of wood were carried out of the yard by the floodwater and floated into the street. The Pudney brothers, who ran the yard, had two identical houses built around this period on the Margaretting Road - Leylands and Langmead.

Another major event of the 1950s was the electrification of the railway line - the section between Shenfield and Chelmsford being done in 1956, with electric passenger services commencing on 11th June. Local passenger services to and from Ingatestone were then generally operated by electric trains, but, as the electrification only extended as far as Chelmsford, steam trains continued to pass through the station hauling trains to and from Clacton and Norwich. These services were themselves replaced by diesel haulage in the early 1960s.

In 1974 local government reorganisation meant that Ingatestone and Fryerning were transferred for administrative purposes from Chelmsford Rural District Council to Brentwood District Council. One of the first, and most unusual, items of business for the new Council was consideration of a proposal to move the Ingatestone stones from Fryerning Lane to Star Lane, which had been suggested as a possible site of their original origin. The idea did not, however, find favour with the councillors and the proposal was rejected.

In 1977 the Silver Jubilee for Elizabeth II was marked, amongst other things, by the provision of some commemorative seating in the High Street and at Fryerning Church. Ten years later, a `hurricane' swept the area, felling two trees in Buttsbury churchyard but leaving much of the rest of the area largely unscathed.

And so we reach the 1990s. It is 80 years since Mrs Wilde was writing. Only 80 years. But so much has changed. It only remains to have a look at Ingatestone today, as a snapshot in time for anyone who comes after, 80 years hence, to tell the history of the village then. But before that we must take a look at one of the great postwar characters in the village - Vera Pemberton.

MISS PEMBERTON

One of the most significant residents in Ingatestone for much of the century was Reverend Bobby Pemberton's daughter, Vera, who founded the Ingatestone Boys' Own Club in February 1919 'to assist in the spiritual, physical and mental development of boys and young men' on the day before her 24th birthday. She was a very active and well-known person in the village.

Miss Pemberton was born in Gosport, Hampshire, in 1895, the eldest of two daughters born to Reverend and Mrs Pemberton. She worked hard at life from an early age both at Sunday School and in teaching the organ. She had started her first boys' group in 1913 at the age of just 18 and during the First World War had spent many hours preparing first aid kits and working for the Red Cross.

When the family moved to Ingatestone she set up the Boys' Own Club from the top class of 11 boys in the church Sunday School, who were put into a separate Bible class. The first meeting took place in the rectory. It was followed by regular Monday evening meetings and the club soon began to take off.

Amongst her many talents, Miss Pemberton was adept at woodwork and made models for the boys in her club. In 1920 the boys held an exhibition of their work at the Working Men's Club (the Community Club), featuring some 200 models. They also played games and studied art and as the 1920s progressed the club expanded rapidly in its new permanent base at the Ingatestone parish room in Stock Lane.

A whole succession of achievements followed. In October 1920 Ingatestone Rovers Football Club was formed from the Boys' Own team. In May 1922 a Communicants Guild was formed, tying in nicely with Miss Pemberton's strong religious views. In September 1924 a club Debating Society was formed, holding regular monthly meetings on a Thursday morning.

In 1925 Ingatestone Rovers separated from the Boys' Own Club because many of its members were now over 20 years old and consequently too old for membership of the club. Miss Pemberton - of course - acted as Rovers' Honorary Treasurer for the next 12 months. In 1926 the football section within the club was re-formed and continued until 1930 when once again the players became too old. A new club, Ingatestone United, was established.

In 1929 Miss Pemberton began the practice of sending Christmas letters to former Club members and in January 1932 she started the Unemployed Club, which ran for just over a year. In 1933 the Boys' Own Club formed an historic link with Tristan da Cunha and in October 1936 the well-known PT class was started. In Christmas that year the Club, at Miss Pemberton's instigation, sent a hamper to a family in Cardiff in line with a scheme for helping distressed areas.

During World War II Miss Pemberton started a waste paper depôt at the rectory and also set up a monthly wives' and mothers' meeting and revived the Communicants Guild which had lapsed in the interim. In 1943 the Club began to run two Bible classes because so many wanted to attend. Old Club members on active service abroad wrote to Miss Pemberton and asked her to pray for them.

Also in 1943 the Club was awarded the Falkner trophy for good citizenship and such was the work of the Club under Miss Pemberton's leadership that it continued from then on to win or be a runner-up in the competition until the award was discontinued in the late 1950s. In 1944 the Club was also runner-up in a competition for best war efforts which was run by the International Youth Council. The waste paper depôt closed in 1946, having collected some 75 tons of paper.

Other charities in the village benefitted from the Boys' Club's fund raising, including Dr Barnado's. House-to-house collections took place along with rummage sales and in 1948 an appeal was launched for food, clothing, books, games and soap for the 'Distress in Europe' campaign. Miss Pemberton was a strong believer in both the National Association of Boys' Clubs (which her club had joined in 1928) and the local Essex Association and the Ingatestone club took part in many of their activities.

Such was the camaraderie generated by the Club that old boys came back for reunions and a great network of members was established. In 1958 the Duke of Gloucester, President of the National Association, paid a visit, which Miss Pemberton was very proud of despite having broken her arm shortly beforehand when falling off a table whilst cleaning the club.

The Club had become so successful that it really needed a headquarters building of its own. Miss Pemberton launched a campaign and asked villagers to subscribe. According to those who knew her 'she was held in such high esteem [that] with voluntary help and grants from the Ministry of Education' her mission was soon accomplished.

For her hard work with the Boys' Own Club, Miss Pemberton was awarded the MBE in June 1959 at the age of 64. The new Club building opened the next year and in 1961 another club was launched: Trueloves Boys' Club, which ran for 22 years until the closure of Trueloves School. This was for handicapped boys, who were encouraged to take part in art and board games and who later visited the main club to play games with the boys there.

There were more campaigns for Barnados, a silver paper collection for some new books for the library in Chelmsford Hospital and a used stamp collection for Guys Hospital, where Miss Pemberton's younger sister, Katherine, was at one time sister in the maternity ward. In 1963 alone 93,304 stamps were collected.

In 1969 the Club celebrated its Golden Jubilee, with 200 members, past and present, meeting up at the Heybridge country club. The following year, the club welcomed its 1000th member.

By the 1970s Miss Pemberton was herself in her 70s and she began to step back slightly from the main activities of the Club. She still did the paperwork and worked a 14-hour day, but by 1979, when aged 84, she could no longer visit the Club and did all her work at her home, St Cedd's in the Market Place, which was virtually an open house to visitors. The previous year, the Duke of Gloucester, son of the previous Duke, had visited the Trueloves Boys' Club, the last major event during her time there.

Miss Pemberton retired from active leadership of the Club in June 1984, having given it 65 years of her very active life. In 1985 she moved to Winifred Dell House in Brentwood and then to Priory Mount Nursing Home in Birkenhead to be near Frances, her niece. She died on 18th October 1992 and a memorial service was held in the parish church to give thanks for her life.

As a speaker at the time put it, "Neither Ingatestone nor the Boys' Club Movement will ever see another Miss Pemberton".

Pemberton Hall

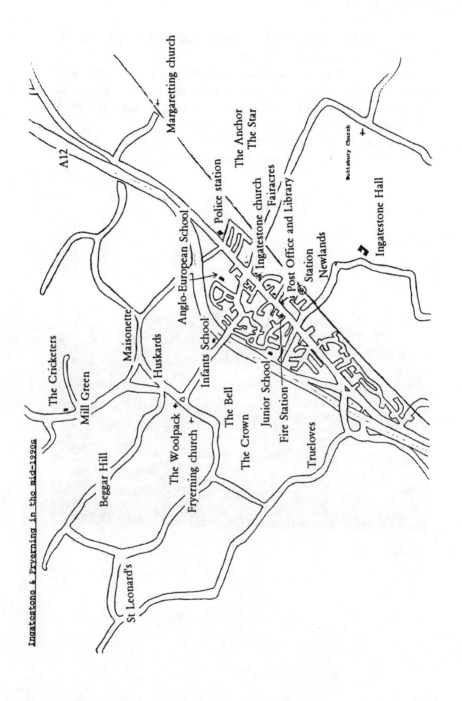

Ingatestone & Fryerning in the mid-1990s

The Cricketers

Mill Green

A12

Margaretting church

Maisonette

Beggar Hill

Huskards

The Woolpack

Fryerning church

St Leonard's

Anglo-European School

Infants School

Police station

Ingatestone church

Fairacres

The Anchor

The Star

The Bell

The Crown

Junior School

Fire Station

Trueloves

Post Office and Library

Station

Newlands

Ingatestone Hall

Buttsbury Church

Since a book like this can only be a snapshot in time in the history of a place and the significant year 2000 is rapidly approaching, it will perhaps be useful to describe for those who come after the appearance of Ingatestone today. This is perhaps best done by a map of the village, reproduced alongside.

The future for the surviving ancient buildings in both villages looks at present a little more rosy than it might have done in the 1960s because of the increasing national awareness of the need for conservation which has gathered momentum over the last 25 years or so. Fortunately, the 1960s redevelopment of Ingatestone's centre was the first large-scale development of the village in its history and this has meant that many of the more important historical buildings have survived. This in turn has allowed the designation of Conservation Areas and the listing of several of the surviving buildings. Numerous buildings in Fryerning are also listed.

There may no longer be 27 pubs in Ingatestone and Fryerning, but those that survive recall former times. The *Crown* has been covered elsewhere, whilst the *Anchor*, internally like the entrance lobby to a grand hotel, has its own bit of history, with the bricks from the original pub being said to have been used to build a pergola in the grounds of Delamas House at Beggar Hill.

The *Star*, erected in about 1480 but subject to a series of alterations since, has been variously a beerhouse, a bakery and a butcher's. The name was transferred from an earlier building, which operated as the *Star* from a property opposite the Community Club. The current building is said to be haunted - the hackles rose on the back of a dog in there once, apparently in response to some super-natural phenomenon, and lights have apparently been turned on and off and doors opened and closed when no-one is around. There is supposed to be a passageway leading from the inn to the church.

The *Bell* is the oldest surviving public house in the village and probably one of the oldest buildings, too. It, and nearby Makrons (now Little Hammonds restaurant), are both shown on John Walker's map of the village in 1601 and the *Bell* is thought to date from c.1450. Its curious angle to the street recalls perhaps an earlier line of the highway. The narrowness of the road here would have given coachmen some difficulty manoeuvring into the yard. The inn sign apparently once bore the Latin motto '*Vivos voco; mortuos plango; fulgura fango* [I call the living; I mourn the dead; I shiver the lightning]', but not any more.

Little Hammonds restaurant itself has an interesting past. It used to be a bakery and has in recent years been in the news for apparent supernatural happenings, including the appearance of a Victorian lady in a long black dress and the denting of a chair cushion as if someone is sitting down on it.

The Whit Wednesday Fair on Fryerning Green in front of the *Woolpack* may have gone, but the pub remains and the Jubilee Tree which has replaced the fair will hopefully be there for many years to come. The old oak tree by the road in the grounds of Fryerning Hall has seen at least 800 years pass by and it may well live to see many more.

Further out, the *Cricketers* inn survives, though no cricket is played there any more, whilst the *Viper* also continues to prosper, despite its remote location. Probably the only pub of that name in the country, it is said to have had delivered during the Second World War a letter addressed simply to: 'The Landlord, *The Viper*, England'. The woods around here, like the paths through the Wid Valley on the Buttsbury side of Ingatestone, remain an important recreation amenity.

So much for the past and the present. But what changes will the future bring to Ingatestone and Fryerning?

With the advent of out-of-town supermarkets, High Streets all over the country have been dying. Ingatestone today battles on with a mixture of shops providing basic provisions for everyday life and others of a surprisingly more specialist nature. It could even be described as 'select' in parts. Will the out-of-town revolution draw shops out of the village centre? This seems unlikely because there is nowhere handily placed to build on and it is Chelmsford and Brentwood that are far more likely to suffer in this regard.

The population will surely continue to grow as the old village continues to cement its position as a popular commuter `town', but the narrow envelope of development land which is available between the railway and the bypass is finite and it may be that one day this development encroaches outside these boundaries, perhaps most likely in the vicinity of the railway station where it would be particularly welcomed by prospective commuters. Hopefully not.

Bell Mead and the new doctor's surgery were constructed only a couple of years before this was written, whilst a new development on the site of the old doctor's in Star Lane was still going on in 1996. The population is also moving around within the locality: in the 1950s the road at Beggar Hill was filled with children playing games and running around; today it is silent.

The village has benefitted to a degree from the influx of new people from outside, with the advent of various dramatic, operatic, and sports societies, which have given additional life to the old historic settlement.

The infrastructure will no doubt change again to meet the demands of the population. The complement of police officers in the village may change, but surely the fire engine will not need to find yet another new home? In the shopping centre there are many more service industry businesses now - estate agents, solicitors and consultants of various kinds.

The transport revolution will continue and the Market Place may be filled before long with electric cars of the kind that analysts are currently predicting will soon be a regular feature of towns throughout the kingdom. As pollution laws become stricter, perhaps locals will turn again to the bicycle as a way of getting around. Perhaps they will walk, since the High Street is not too big to enable one to do that in comfort. A return to horse-riding would seem to be unlikely?

Outside the village the farmlands may well play host to some different crops, as European Community subsidies, `set-aside' rules and environmentally-sensitive farming policies continue to be developed.

The computer, too, will no doubt play more of a part in our everyday lives as time goes on.

Predicting the future is risky, because the predictions are invariably wrong. Had Mrs Wilde predicted two world wars and a transport revolution within 30 years of her book being published she would no doubt have been laughed out of court.

Whatever the future brings to Ingatestone, good luck to whoever comes to the village, and particularly to the person, perhaps not yet born, who many decades hence writes the next chapter of the village's long and eventful history.

The Viper

SELECT BIBLIOGRAPHY

Braddon, Mary Elizabeth (Mrs Maxwell) *Lady Audley's Secret*, Oxford University Press, 1987 (originally 1861-2)

Buckler, George *Twenty-Two of the Churches of Essex*, Bell & Daldy, 1856

Coe, R. A. *A Postcard from Ingatestone*, R. A. Coe, 1989

Davies, C. S. L. *and* Garnett, Jane, *editors Wadham College*, Wadham College, 1994 *Dictionary of National Biography*

Edwards, A. C. *and* Newton, K. *The Walkers of Hanningfield*, Buckland Publications, 1984

Edwards, A. C. *John Petre*, Regency Press, 1975

Emmison, F. G. *Tudor Secretary*, Longmans, 1961

Emmison, F. G. *Tudor Food and Pastimes*, Ernest Benn, 1964

Essex Record Office, *Old Thorndon Hall*, Essex Record Office, 1972

Forster, Stewart *The Catholic Church in Ingatestone*, John Glyn, 1982

Fryerning Church guidebook

Harvard, Lesley C. *Country Chronicles*, Ian Henry, 1992

Hewitt, Gordon *A History of the Diocese of Chelmsford*, Chelmsford Diocesan Board of Finance, 1984

Ingatestone Church guidebook

Ingatestone Hall guidebook

Langford, Kenneth *Ingatestone and District in old picture postcards*, European Library, 1992

Langford, Kenneth *Edward Freeman Hudson (1906-1989)*, University of Essex, 1995

Lemmon, David *The Book of Essex Cricketers*, Breedon Books, 1994

Lemmon, David *and* Marshall, Mike *Essex County Cricket Club*, Kingswood Press, 1987

Marriage, John *Barging into Chelmsford*, Ian Henry, 1997

Marriage, John *Bygone Brentwood*, Phillimore, 1990

Miles, Sarah *A Right Royal Bastard*, Macmillan, 1993

Notes on the Thanksgiving Service for the life of Miss E. V. Pemberton

Petre, M. D. *The Ninth Lord Petre*, The Society for Promoting Christian Knowledge, 1928

Pevsner, Nikolaus *Buildings of England, Essex*, Penguin, 1954 (1988 reprint)

Sale, Charles *Korty*, Ian Henry, 1986

Smith, J. R. *The Speckled Monster*, Essex Record Office, 1987

Wilde, Mrs E .E. with Mrs Archibald Christy *Ingatestone and the Essex Great Road, With Fryerning*, Oxford University Press, 1913

Various copies of Ingatestone and Fryerning parish magazines and various publications by Brentwood Borough Council, the Essex Record Office, Ingatestone & Fryerning Parish Council and the Ingatestone & Fryerning Historical and Archæological Society.